BRANDING
FIRST
VOL.2

SP
SendPoints

BRANDING FIRST VOL.2
Copyright©2011 by Sendpoints Publishing Co., Limited

SendPoints

Publisher: Lin Gengli
Editor in Chief: Lin Shijian
Editorial Director: Jimmy Chai
Executive Editor: Ellyse Ho
Design Director: Lin Shijian
Executive Designer: Liu Minting

Address: Room 15A Block 9 Tsui Chuk Garden,Wong Tai Sin,
          Kowloon,Hongkong
Tel: (86)-20-89095121
Fax: (86)-20-89095206
Email: info@sendpoint.com.cn
Website: www.sendpoint.com.cn

Distributed by Guangzhou Sendpoints Book Co., Ltd.
Sales Manager: Peng YangHui(China)   Limbo(International)
Guangzhou Tel: (86)-02-89095121
Beijing   Tel: (86)-10-84139071
Shanghai   Tel: (86)-21-63523469
Email: export@sendpoint.com.cn
Website: www.sendpoint.com.cn

ISBN 978-988-15624-3-2

BRANDING FIRST VOL.2

BRAND RENEW	NEW BRAND

BRANDING FIRST VOL.2

PREFACE

What is brand?

A brand can represent a person, a product even an enterprise as an invisible property. It exists in the mankind brain naturally meaning the public cognition and understanding of a brand, which not only deeply influences the people's consuming impression and habit, but also leads the social trend as well as cultural development. Branding becomes more and more important to promote company's awareness, engage the consumers, and distinguish itself from others in the fierce competition. From the product construction to brand planning, enterprise environment packaging to image packaging, commercial design to brand identity design, the enterprise's awareness of brand is increasing by and by.

New brand requires creativity

Today, the creativity has been an important driving force for the enterprise development and society advancement. As the consumers' demand and aesthetic appreciation improve higher, the start-up brand or established brand has been confronted with a new challenge. Everyday thousands of new brands emerge around the world, just like the new born baby, which injects more fresh blood into the market. However, not every new brand will survive in the competition, a brand lack in creativity and isn't in accord with the facts will be forgotten easily and eventually leads the enterprise to failure just like a flash in the pan. One has less competitiveness who wants to gain a foothold in the market needs to distinguish itself with a creative brand image. Survival of the fittest, only the brand in accordance with character of the enterprise can catch the eyes and sympathy of public and provide strong support to the enterprise development.

Renew brand also requires creativity. ◇◇◇

As people's appreciation and concern about the brand identity become more and more critical, the brand redesign seems unavoidable to enterprise development. Our life change everyday, the outdated fixed brand is doomed to eliminate gradually in the fierce competition. When an established brand starts to become laggard, outdated and unaccommodated to the society trend, competition, consumer culture as well as the strategic adjustment, the redesign of brand becomes an objective demand and an inevitable result of the enterprise construction and development. The redesign identity will help to correct the former brand and make it up to date and more energetic. The redesign usually is executed within the slight change in color, material and shape, which enable the consumer to realize the correction and meantime accept it. While other redesign will extend to the name, logo, package, product and ads, etc. and reposition it through changing its previous brand identity. Whether the fine adjustments or the extensive alterations, all the redesign should be based on the market-oriented strategy and precondition that leading brand is built up by creativity rather than blind pursuit. ◇◇◇◇◇◇◇◇◇◇◇◇◇

◇◇◇

"Branding First Vol.2" is the continuance of "Branding First". This book covers across designs of clothes, food, dining, electron, media and individual, which aims to introduce the reader the latest brand identity designs all over the world. Among these selected works, some featured with bold color, some with creative format, and some with simplicity style, highlighting the brand character, the unique conception and technique of expression of designers. Moreover, it also collects series of rebranding designs, among which some are only slightly altered based on its former brand identity, some are repositioned to change its former established image, while some are renamed and changed its appearance. ◇◇◇◇◇◇◇◇◇◇◇◇◇◇◇◇◇◇

Through the avant-garde brand identity designs in this book, you can know how designers merge into the enterprise tradition and style to create successful brand redesign works. Besides, you can perceive the subtle link between the new brands and renewing brands. What's creativity? How to be creative? How one can combine the creativity with reality? Then this book will be the answers through plenty of brand design cases. ◇◇◇

Lastly, we avail ourselves of this opportunity to express our sincere thanks to the design studios and designers who contribute to this book, without whom there will be no "Branding First Vol.2". Thank you! ◇◇

◇◇◇

◇◇◇

◇◇◇

BRANDING FIRST ◇◇◇◇◇◇◇◇◇◇◇◇◇

VOL.2

CONTENT

BRAND RENEW

BELMACZ

Belmacz is a London based jewelry company. The identity re-design relates to the process in which raw minerals and diamonds are more and more refined until they become a piece of jewelry. On their journey from the mine to the jewelry shop, those materials go through many hands and constantly change location. Not only the raw materials travel also the final pieces of jewelry are often passed on from one generation to the next, given away as presents, got stolen or auctioned. For this reason the new Belmacz identity works cover many different items and media. Every shape that has been cut out on one item of communication re-appears on another. For example a shape missing on a business card can re-appear on a carrier bag.

belmacz

Before

After

STUDIO: Mind Design   CREATIVE DIRECTOR: Holger Jacobs   DESIGNER: Mind Design

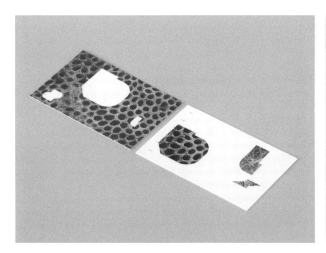

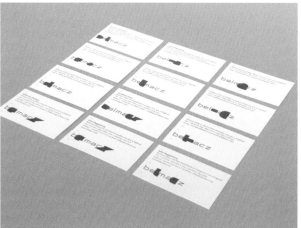

CLIENT: Belmacz   COUNTRY: UK

NAILME

nailme

NAIL ME

NAIL ME

"Getting nailed" can insinuate a very sexual remark. Nail Me is a salon based in Vancouver Canada who specialises in manicures and pedicures. Each section of the branding is very direct and contains sexual innuendoes.

HOW DO YOU WANT TO GET NAILED?

Artistic Spa Manicure - 60min - $39
Includes: hand and arm exfoliation, massage, mask, cuticles and nails trimmed to perfection and polished w/nail art

Classic Manicure - 45min - $27
Includes: shape, hand exfoliation cuticles and nails trimmed, massage and polish

"Man"icure Treatment - 30min - $27
Nails are neatly trimmed, rough spots smoothed

Teen Manicure -30min - $25
Our professional nail technicians will shape, massage and polish your hands. Choose from the latest nail fashions by OPI & Creative with a sparkling gemstone.

Artistic Spa Pedicure -75min - $69
A spa pedicure with the same great results as the treatment pedicure with an added exfoliation, and nail art.

Hot Stone Pedicure -75min - $69
Our treatment pedicure enhanced with heated lava stones are massage into your foot and lower leg. The soothing effects of the stones combined with the deep penetration of essential oils offer "simply the best experience"

NAILME

GET NAILED 10 TIMES
AND RECEIVE YOUR NEXT APPOINTMENT WITH US FREE

NAILME

Our Pleasurex

with pleasurex

STUDIO: Hangar 18 Creative   CREATIVE DIRECTOR: Chris Cavill   DESIGNER: Chris Cavill

CLIENT: Nail Me Salon (Manicure/pedicure)   COUNTRY: UK

GIRL SCOUTS OF THE USA

The Girl Scouts recently revised both their programming and advertising to better engage girls today. To support this shift, they approached us to reassess their overall brand identity. They asked for a mark that represented the best of what they could be by reinforcing their young, energetic and girlish strength, while still being sensitive to their rich history.

Before

After

gs

c

STUDIO: The Original Champions of Design   **CREATIVE DIRECTOR:** Jennifer Kinon, Bobby C, Martin Jr

Building girls of courage, confidence, and character, who make the world a better place.

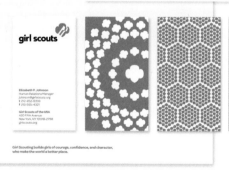

CLIENT: Girl Scouts of the USA   COUNTRY: U.S.A

VPRO

VPRO is a well-known broadcasting network in the Netherlands. It stands for creativity, freedom and intellect. In the Dutch broadcasting system 17 networks are mixed over three channels. Therefore it is very important to have a distinctive and clear branding.

The new logo for the VPRO consists of the letters VPRO in a newly developed font, with the round shapes in the 'p' and 'o' intersected by two triangles. The logo has been designed for flexible use, with more than one billion forms which can varied through color differences, gradients, patterns and radiations. These variations are across different mediums and in between programs, as identity.

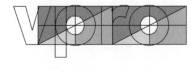

STUDIO: Thonik   CREATIVE DIRECTOR: Thonik   CLIENT: Vpro

COUNTRY: The Netherlands

Armadillo
Janus Metz

AMSTERDAM ROYAL ZOO ARTIS

Artis is the oldest zoo in Holland and lies just in the centre of Amsterdam.
Artis is much more than just a zoo: it's a city park, it has educational programs,
during summer there's a cultural event. That's the reason for not making a typical
'zoo-identity', in safari colors and funny typefaces. Also Van lennep decided not to
use any color in typography, and the only color lies in photography and illustrations.
During the process they decided to re-use old typography they found on a fence in
the Park. It has a typical Amsterdam feel and also gives a feel of the rich history of
Artis. They combined it with the typeface 'Simple' to give it a contemporary look (Only
for the logo). For texts and info they used the 'Omnes', a modern good readable
typeface with a subtle personality.

CREATIVE DIRECTOR: Van lennep   **DESIGNER:** Van lennep   **CLIENT:** Natura Artis Magistra

COUNTRY: The Netherlands

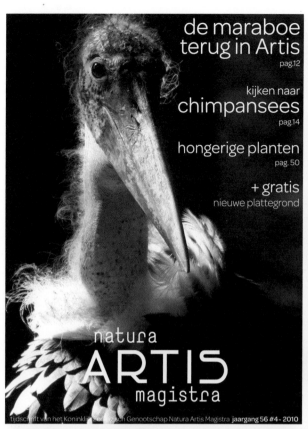

de maraboe
terug in Artis
pag.12

kijken naar
chimpansees
pag.14

hongerige planten
pag. 50

+ gratis
nieuwe plattegrond

natura
ARTIS
magistra

tijdschrift van het Koninklijk Zoölogisch Genootschap Natura Artis Magistra jaargang 56 #4- 2010

winter
avonden
dieren in het donker

Artis
open tot
21 uur

elke avond een speciale gast
zaterdag 11 december
zaterdag 18 december
vrijdag 24 december

vrijdag
24 december
een speciaal
programma in
het Planetarium

❄ een levende kerststal
❄ lekkere stampotten en glühwein
❄ liederen van het kerstkoor

avondrondleidingen
achter de schermen

natura
ARTIS
magistra

giraffen veroveren
savanne
nu samen met zebra's. gnoes,
springbokken en parelhoenders. pag. 14

hoe ver kun je kijken
in het heelal?
pag. 50

gratis
bomenkaart

natura
ARTIS
magistra

tijdschrift van het Koninklijk Zoölogisch Genootschap Natura Artis Magistra jaargang 56 #3- 2010

geboren en verwacht
lepelaar, mara, miereneter, giraf, zeeleeuw…
pag. 28

welke wilde gasten
heeft Artis?
pag. 42

swingende
ZOOmeravonden
JAZZ, POËZIE, BIJZONDERE VERHALEN
pag. 14

natura
ARTIS
magistra

tijdschrift van het Koninklijk Zoölogisch Genootschap Natura Artis Magistra jaargang 56 #2- 2010

lidmaatschap

natura
ARTIS
magistra

expected
in June
artis.nl

natura
ARTIS
magistra

image: David Barlow Photography/Pioneer Productions from de series: In the Womb

juli

goudwanggibbon
Nomascus gabriellae

De goudwanggibbon lijkt wel te vliegen als hij zich van boom tot boom door het Zuidoost-Aziatische regenwoud slingert. Op opperarbeid kan hij afstanden van maar liefst tien meter vrij overend overbruggen. Onderin gaan plukt hij belangrijke nog vruchten af, zelfs vast over arenmingeleke uit de boom. Op de grond maakt hij op twee poten, de velerearm lange armen hoog boven het hoofd gestel. Het schoon houdt hij te veterleer vechten. De zachte handschuit huid verbreden van een waarheid van een harde gelegen apen maakt kleine mensen en het handvangelenk gevangelen, de volwassen lichaard van boven met pale zwarte in van. Het mossische de geboren mosdes boschuite goor overleeft dije even van het buit. Slei naar exporten. De satele contact mes is boter man ze mouse schult bijget verg deze het darrkers waruit. Zo houden ze liechtele's vrege zegingeden weigulichun waarstomtaruni. De door is om lage vraag in Artis ta'n ones. Nacht als ontwikeprojecten het gevorg helport. Vlei zager zo de viezmitike giftlenis actuel weg uit hun zal bonsun schen hij blauer ze zitterd in hun favoriete beschboom.

natura
ARTIS
magistra

THE MUNICIPALITY AMSTERDAM

The municipality Amsterdam wanted to show clearly who she is. More than 50 different identities are brought back to one strong and univocal style in which all people concerned can identify. The style of Amsterdam is misleading simple with the three red Saint Andrew's crosses as eye-catcher and offers much space for adding own identity characteristics for every district. This project was done in collaboration with Eden Design and Communication.

Gemeente Amsterdam
Dienst Economische Zaken

Gemeente Amsterdam
Dienst Waterleiding

Gemeente Amsterdam
ProjectManagement Bureau

100y100m	100y66m	100y33m	100c
100y33c	100y66c	100y100c	100c66y
100c33y	100c	100c33m	100c66m
100m100c	100m66c	100m33c	100m

STUDIO: Thonik   CREATIVE DIRECTOR: Thonik   DESIGNER: Thonik

city of Amsterdam
20.000 civil servants
3 billion euro annual budget
55 services and boroughs
~~55 logo's~~

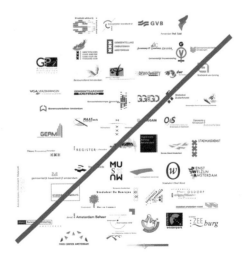

CLIENT: The municipality Amsterdam   COUNTRY: The Netherlands

VISIT NORDKYN

The Nordkyn peninsula is the furthermost part of Europe and accommodates two municipalities (Gamvik and Lebesby) in the county of Finnmark, Norway. The two municipalities developed a joint marketing strategy for their investment in tourism, 'Visit Nordkyn'. Neue Design Studio was given the task to unite and promote "Visit Nordkyn" as one tourist destination.

The visual identity is based on two main ingredients; newly developed payoff - "Where nature rules" - and weather statistics from The Norwegian Meteorological Institute. A feed of weather statistics effects the logo to change when the direction of the wind or the temperature changes. On the website, the logo updates every five minute. They developed a logo generator where "Visit Nordkyn" can download their logo to the exact weather conditions of that particular moment.

NORDKYN
DER
NATUREN
RÅR

NORDKYN
WHERE
NATURE
RULES

NORDKYN
26.10.10
SW 8M/S
-10.3°

ULTRA-
MAGNETIC

71°08'02"N

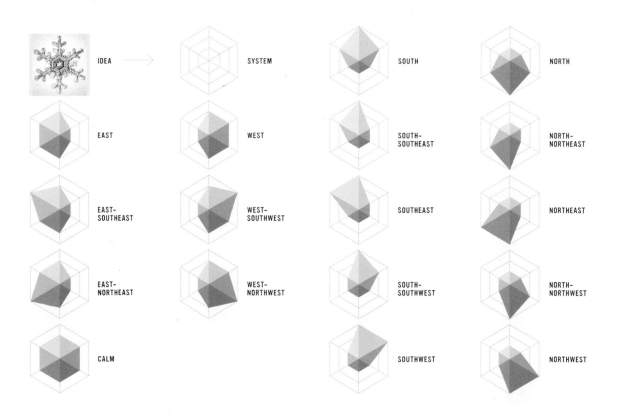

STUDIO: Neue Design Studio   **DESIGNER:** Neue Design Studio   **CLIENT:** Visit Nordkyn

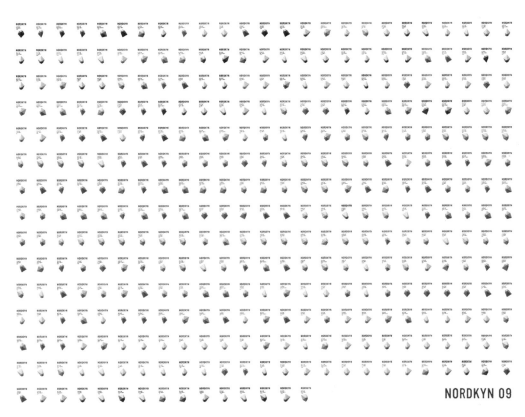

NORDKYN 09

COUNTRY: Norway

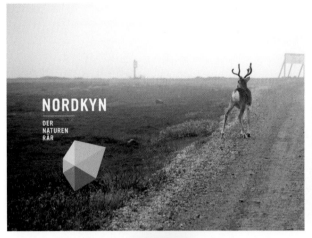

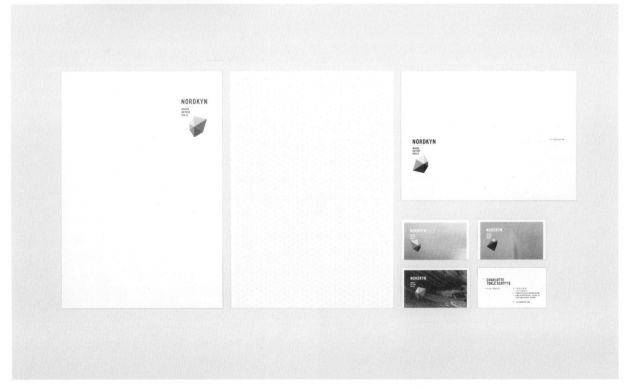

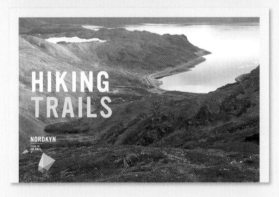

FRANKFURT HAHN AIRPORT

Corporate design for Frankfurt Hahn Airport. The new appearance's main element is a three-colored word mark, based on a slightly modified set of the font Magda Clean OT.

Further stylistic elements complete the young airport's corporate design: Out of some of the font's basic elements, several simple, generally understandable pictograms have been developed. They support the design of orientation and information graphics that have to work in an international environment. Additionally, over 20 graphical characters, from aircraft captain to cargo staff member, were established for targeted communication in different business areas.

So far, business stationery, image brochure, terminal plans and flight schedules, fair stands and a style guide have been developed.

Before   After

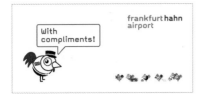

STUDIO: Projekttriangle Design Studio   CREATIVE DIRECTOR: Martin Grothmaak, Prof. Jürgen Späth

DESIGNER: Franziska Strantz, Nagisa Oki-Fries, Daisuke Nitta   **CLIENT:** Flughafen Frankfurt-Hahn GmbH   **COUNTRY:** Germany

UNITED STATES POSTAL SERVICE

Identity design for United States Postal Service. The retro feel, in addition to playing up a popular aesthetic, is a cultural homage to an earlier 1950s-era nostalgia, a pre-internet and pre-cell phone age. The new look is warm, inviting, and makes people want to grab a pen and a sheet of paper and see what that old friend's been up. His inspiration came largely from vintage gas station signage, and the bird is a nod to the notion of sending something via the antiquated method of "carrier pigeon."

Before

After

CREATIVE DIRECTOR: Matt Chase   DESIGNER: Matt Chase   CLIENT: Student Project

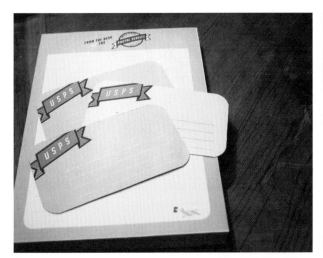

COUNTRY: U.S.A

THE MARMALADE PANTRY

A popular and upmarket café that prides itself on offering 'good things to eat', The Marmalade Pantry was preparing to move to its new premises at Singapore's premier shopping gallery, the Ion Ochard. &Larry worked closely with client and interior designer to create an organic and memorable identity that would go hand-in-hand with the branding and environment.

STUDIO: &Larry   CREATIVE DIRECTOR: Larry Peh   DESIGNER: Lee Weicong

CLIENT: The Marmalade Group   COUNTRY: Singapore

BREITENTHALER

The Austrian company "Mobelbau Breitenthaler" stands for creative design combined with craftsmanship, for extreme aesthetic appeal and a true passion for materials, forms and colors. The result is timeless, beautiful furniture whose focus is always on the material: wood. With the renewed branding, moodley brand identity has set up a monument to this timeless material. It equally unifies all values described above that the company stands for.

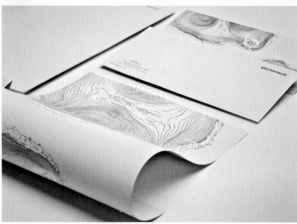
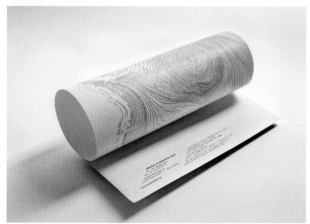

STUDIO: moodley brand identity　　　**CREATIVE DIRECTOR:** Albert Handler　　　**DESIGNER:** Anouk Rehorek

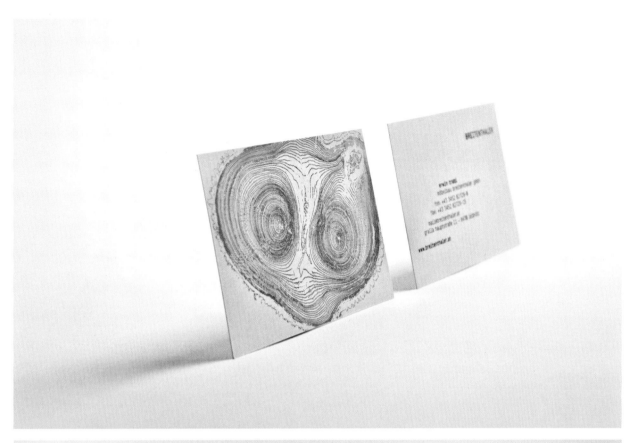

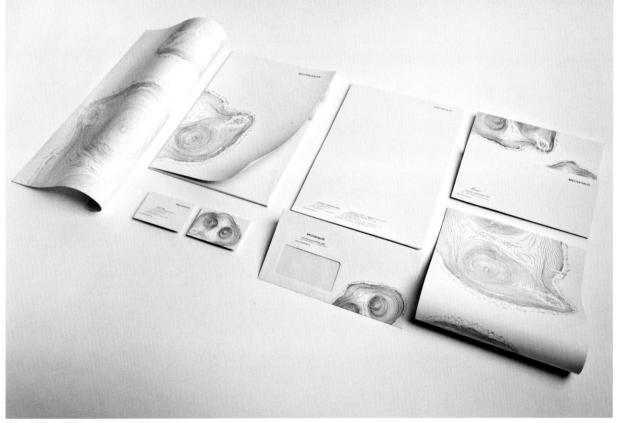

CLIENT: Möbelbau Breitenthaler   COUNTRY: Austria

PRONTO REBRANDING

Pronto is a chain of Italian restaurants based in Moscow. The logo refers to Roman mythology, Mercury's winged hat which supports the meaning of restaurant's name. At the same time, illustrations help to convey the peaceful and prepossessing atmosphere of the place.

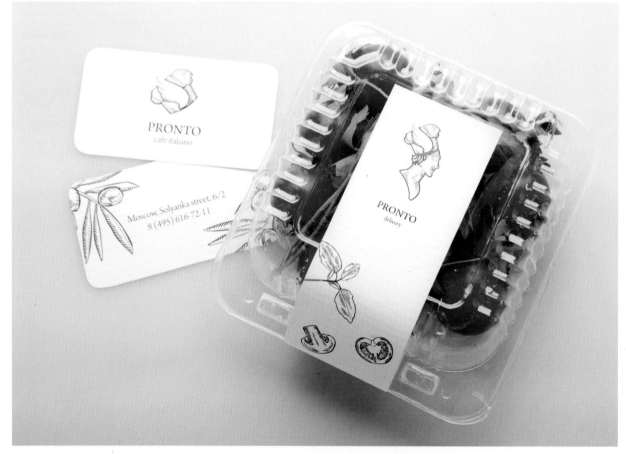

DESIGNER: Daria Karpenko   **COUNTRY**: Russia

'NORWEGIAN SHIPOWNERS' ASSOCIATION IDENTITY

The objective of the Norwegian Shipowners' Association (NSA) is to look after its members' interests. Their logo was outdated and they had no coherent system for their members to present themselves visually. This constitutes the concept of the new identity, with an iconic representation of NSAs' universe. The solution is bold and forward-looking, and underscores NSA as a competent and global actor. Juxtaposing Norwegian and English in the logotype also eliminates their previous need for multiple logos.

STUDIO: Neue Design

DESIGNER: Lars Havard Dahlstrom, Benjamin Stenmarck, Oystein Haugseth

CLIENT: Norwegian Shipowners' Association

PURE IDENTITY REDESIGN

The PURE Water Company has a special system that utilizes the municipal water supply network providing drinking water of the highest quality. The company wanted to redesign their identity to convey the environmental benefits of their product. A communication concept was developed which enhances the core benefits of the product through four statements: RE.THINK, RE.FILL, RE.FINE and RE.FRESH. The logo was redesigned to create a clean and modern look, and the characters were redrawn to work horizontally and vertically. Product design by Scandinavian Design Group and website by apt.no.

CLIENT: The PURE Water Company   COUNTRY: Norway

S+ S+ S+ S+

SCHMITT+SOHN AUFZÜGE **SCHMITT+SOHN AUFZÜGE** **SCHMITT+SOHN AUFZÜGE** **SCHMITT+SOHN AUFZÜGE**

100 Jahre Erfa
1.360 leidensch
Mitarbeiter, 1 p
krönte Designs
80.000 gebaut
anlagen, 24 St
Bereitschaft a
im Jahr. Für lang anhal-
tende Partnerschaften.

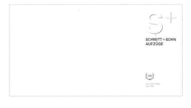

STUDIO: Projekttriangle Design Studio   **CREATIVE DIRECTOR:** Martin Grothmaak, Prof. Jürgen Späth

SCHMITT + SOHN ELEVATORS

Projekttriangle was given the task of developing a new image for Schmitt + Sohn elevators, a company that works all over Europe. As part of this new visual identity a 100-page company brochure was produced. In this brochure, which illustrates the values, products and references of the company, it is the staff that creates the identity of the company. Each subject is represented by one employee who gives it a face and introduces it with a personal quote.

Besides the design as well as the portrait and documentary photography Projekttriangle is also responsible for the text and the concept.

Before

After

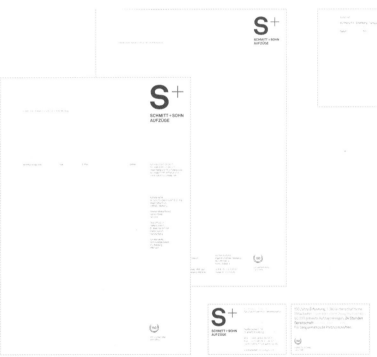

DESIGNER: Franz Stämmele
Daisuke Nitta
Theresa Brandau

CLIENT: Aufzugswerke M. Schmitt + Sohn GmbH & Co

COUNTRY: Germany

ERGO

ERGO is one of Europe's biggest insurance groups, taking in 18 billion Euros in insurance premiums every year. ERGO is active in over 30 countries around the world, mostly in Europe and Asia.

ERGO aims to be perceived as a trustworthy, reliable adviser that speaks to its clients at eye level and conveys competence and clarity. "To insure is to understand" is the slogan for the modern, customer-oriented service provider.

The new look and feel of the brand is as unique as it is attention-grabbing. The main design element in all communication media is the "Flow", which harmonizes with the imagery and also appears in branded environments. The diversity of design forms increases the range of flexible design options and reflects the individuality of ERGO clients: ERGO adapts to fit its customers.

STUDIO: MetaDesign AG **CREATIVE DIRECTOR:** Robert A. Schaefer **DESIGNER:** Anja Allen **CLIENT:** ERGO **COUNTRY:** Germany
Petra Vogt

PROVINCE OF NOORD-HOLLAND

Organizations which act in the interests of a number of groups are complex.

Clear communication is therefore essential within this complexity. After period of reorganizations, the Province of Noord-Holland wished to create a clearer profile towards citizens, visitors and businesses.

Edenspiekermann first established, along with the province, a number of identity values. The new house style with a new logo arose from that. This made the communications of the Province of Noord-Holland more straightforward and efficient.

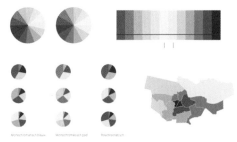

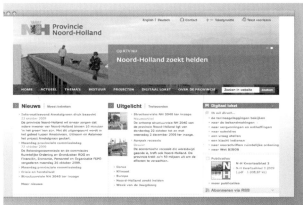

STUDIO: Edenspiekermann   **DESIGNER:** Marieke Griffioen / Guus Pot / Hannah Manneke   **CLIENT:** The Province of Noord-Holland   **COUNTRY:** The Netherlands

PAIN PLAT

The aim is to redesign a Norwegian product for the French market. Flat-bread is usually eaten together with other traditional Norwegian dishes, and is just a flat bread that doesn't really taste much. To make it interesting for the French market (as they have quite enough quality bread already), they rebranded it as a healthy snack that comes together with three different dips. they focused on creating a traditional yet modern look, marketing the product for the French market as a healthy Norwegian delicacy.

DESIGNER: Mikael Floysand, Sofie Platou, Julie Elise Hauge, Bendik Hoibraaten   **CLIENT:** School assignment

COUNTRY: Norway

CONFECTIONERY PACKAGE

"Einem" Union is the oldest Union in Russia, manufacturing confectionery products. The aim was to redesign package and wrappers for three well-known sorts of sweets, produced by Einem: Belochka (Squirrel), Mishka na Severe (Northern Bear) and Zolotoy Petushok (Golden Cockerel). The main conditions were to make the package eco-friendly and to save special way of wrapping sweet. Therefore, paper for package was made out of newspapers, and minimum amount of glue was used.

DESIGNER: Daria Karpenko   **COUNTRY:** Russia

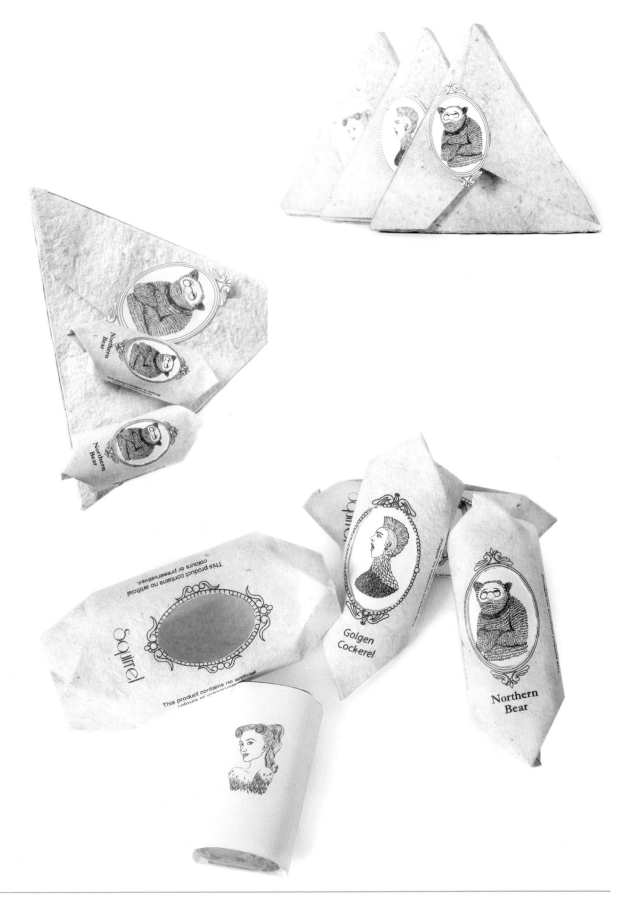

FEEL FILMS

Based in the heart of London's West End, Feel is a production company that produces work for advertising, film and television. Their existing identity system was convoluted and dated. Colt was briefed to create an identity that focused on modernity and simplicity. The consultancy delivered a design that uses recycled stock, with a foil-blocked, linear word mark. These elements also form the basis of the new website.

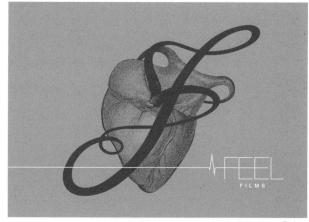

Before

After

STUDIO: Colt   DESIGNER: Alex Chappell   CLIENT: Alex Chappell   COUNTRY: UK

ITV STUDIOS

When ITV Productions became ITV Studios, they needed a new identity to reflect their positioning as the world's leading creator and distributor of multi-platform entertainment. The flexible animation reflects both the variety of outputs and the emotive ups and downs of watching quality TV. It also uses colors from the previous identities of Granada and ITV Productions coming together in one. The brand is now internationally recognized as a major creative force, and ITV Studios has been adopted as the umbrella brand for all ITV's sales, productions and international sectors.

STUDIO: Mammal Ltd. CREATIVE DIRECTOR: Joe Hosp DESIGNER: Ollie Thomas CLIENT: ITV Studios COUNTRY: UK
Grace Chao
Nick Shea

16&PREGNANT DAYTIME

STUDIO: *Pogo*

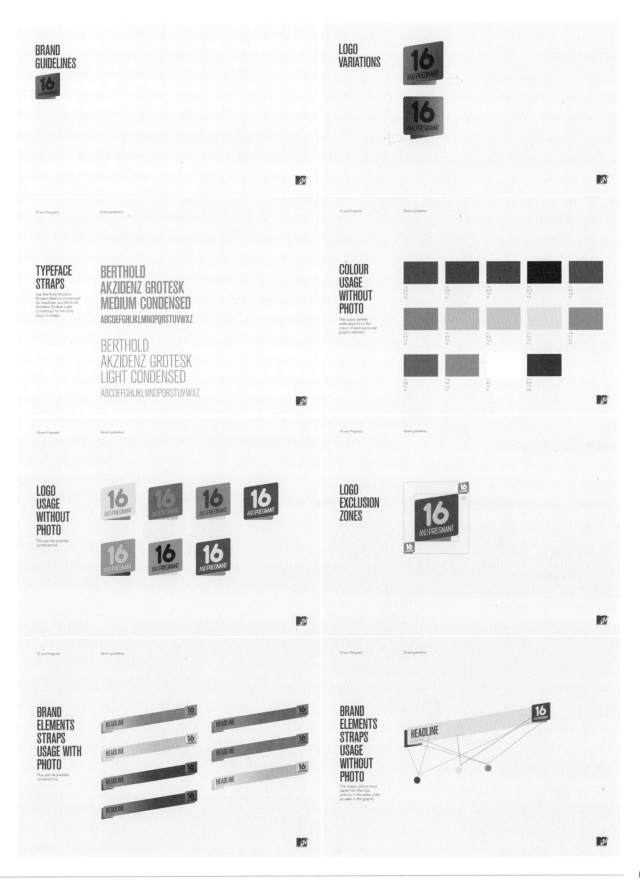

BRAND GUIDELINES

LOGO VARIATIONS

TYPEFACE STRAPS

Use Berthold Akzidenz Grotesk Medium Condensed for headlines, and Berthold Akzidenz Grotesk Light Condensed for the body copy, on straps.

BERTHOLD
AKZIDENZ GROTESK
MEDIUM CONDENSED
ABCDEFGHIJKLMNOPQRSTUVWXZ

BERTHOLD
AKZIDENZ GROTESK
LIGHT CONDENSED
ABCDEFGHIJKLMNOPQRSTUVWXZ

COLOUR USAGE WITHOUT PHOTO

The colour palette while depend on the colour of each particular graphic element.

LOGO USAGE WITHOUT PHOTO

This are the possible combinations.

LOGO EXCLUSION ZONES

BRAND ELEMENTS STRAPS USAGE WITH PHOTO

This are the possible combinations.

HEADLINE

BRAND ELEMENTS STRAPS USAGE WITHOUT PHOTO

The straps colours must came from the logo colours, in the same order as seen in the graphic.

HEADLINE

SATURDAYS 22:30
PREMIERES 25 SEPTEMBER
16 AND PREGNANT

16
AND PREGNANT

SADDLE PANTS
BECOME A HORSE AND TURN YOUR BABY INTO A COWBABY!

WATCH 16 AND PREGNANT AND
SEE WHAT IT'S REALLY LIKE.

MTV16ANDPREGNANT.COM

SATURDAYS 22:30
PREMIERES 25 SEPTEMBER
16 AND PREGNANT

16
AND PREGNANT

KANGAROO HOODIE
YOUR STYLE AND YOUR BABY ARE SECURE!

WATCH 16 AND PREGNANT AND
SEE WHAT IT'S REALLY LIKE.

MTV16ANDPREGNANT.COM

SATURDAYS 22:30
PREMIERES 25 SEPTEMBER
16 AND PREGNANT

16
AND PREGNANT

CANVAS DRESS
ENCOURAGE YOUR LITTLE ARTIST AND WEAR HIS DESIGNS.

WATCH 16 AND PREGNANT AND
SEE WHAT IT'S REALLY LIKE.

MTV16ANDPREGNANT.COM

AP.ART REBRAND

AP.ART is an Architecture Studio based in Lisbon, Portugal, born in 2011.

The objective was to create a dynamic symbol reflecting the different views of each individual architect that take part in the project.

The branding idea starts with the general idea of a building: a roof and four walls, and then makes a visual game between some concepts: Straight Vs Plain; Space Vs Module; Concrete Vs Abstract; Perception Vs Perspective; Two-Dimensional Vs Three-Dimensional; Scientific Vs Artistic, concepts belonging to the world of architecture.

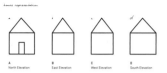

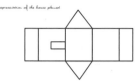

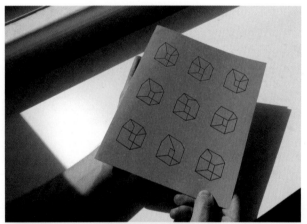

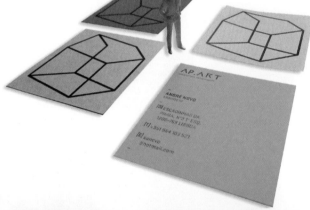

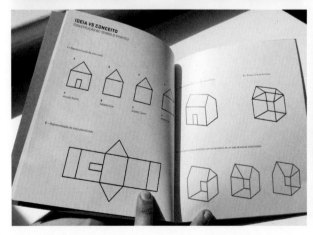

STUDIO: Francisco Elias   **DESIGNER:** Francisco Elias   **CLIENT:** AP.ART Arquitectura Projecto(.)Art / Med Escolha Mediação Imobiliária. LDA.

MED ESCOLHA

MED ESCOLHA   ED ESCOLHA   M D ESCOLHA

ME ESCOLHA   ED ESCOLHA   MED SCOLHA

MED E COLHA   MED ES OLHA   MED ESC LHA

MED ESCO HA   MED ESCOL A   MED ESCOLH

MED ESCOLHA REBRAND

Med Escolha is a young dynamic and entrepreneurial company, composed by a team lead by experienced and knowledgeable professionals in the field of real estate.

The construction of the graphic symbol and logo appears as a simultaneous process. The typography used in the logo appears as building elements of the symbol.

The graphic objective was to exploit the relation between the brand and their application in a unique way.

COUNTRY: Portugal

BARSI MARMI BRAND REDESIGN

BarsiMarmi asked michbold to rethink its corporate image to update the identity to a worldwide market, especially targeting the redesign to architectural and interior design studios.

After

Before

STUDIO: Michbold   **CREATIVE DIRECTOR:** Michele Boldi   **DESIGNER:** Luca Canaletti   **CLIENT:** Barsi Marmi

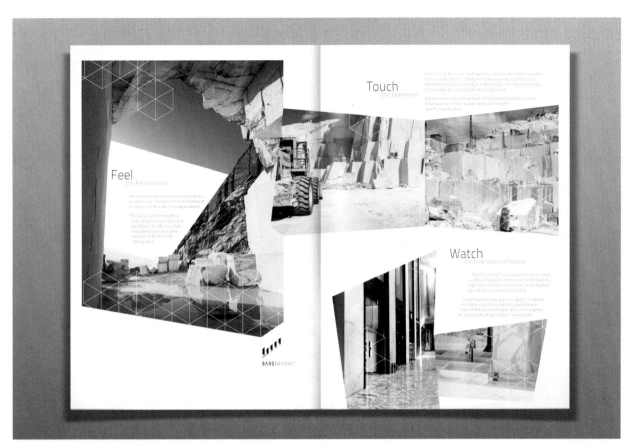

COUNTRY: Italy

NEW BRAND

RIVERPARK

Riverpark's menu suggests there is nothing they wouldn't consider putting on a fork if it surprised, delighted and satisfied their guests. That attitude formed the basis for the own design strategy as it asked, "What would we put on a fork to feed the visual appetite?" The answer, classic wood-cut line drawings, from farm fresh beets to fat-happy cherubs, whole fish to meat cleavers, martini glasses to classic typewriters and exploding champagne bottles, all playfully balanced onto the north-end of an upright fork and letter-pressed into the surface of fine toothy papers.

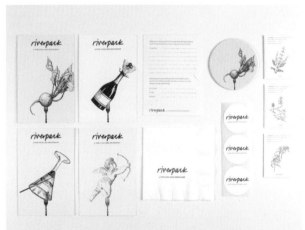

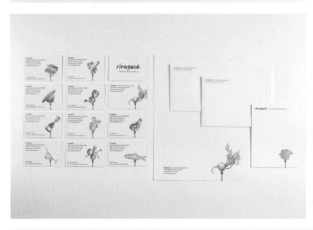

STUDIO: Opto Design   **CREATIVE DIRECTOR:** John Klotnia   **DESIGNER:** Masha Zolotarsky, Svenja Knoedler, Mika Osborne

CLIENT: Riverpark   **COUNTRY:** U.S.A

HIMALAYAS ART MUSEUM

The museum looks like a huge box with plenty elements and unified content. The changing logo not only can present the development concept of Himalayas Art Museum through different aspects, such as easiness, youth, communication, consideration, collection and distribution, but also can add more symbol under the basic one according to personal preference, inviting more people to participate in the design process of museum identity.

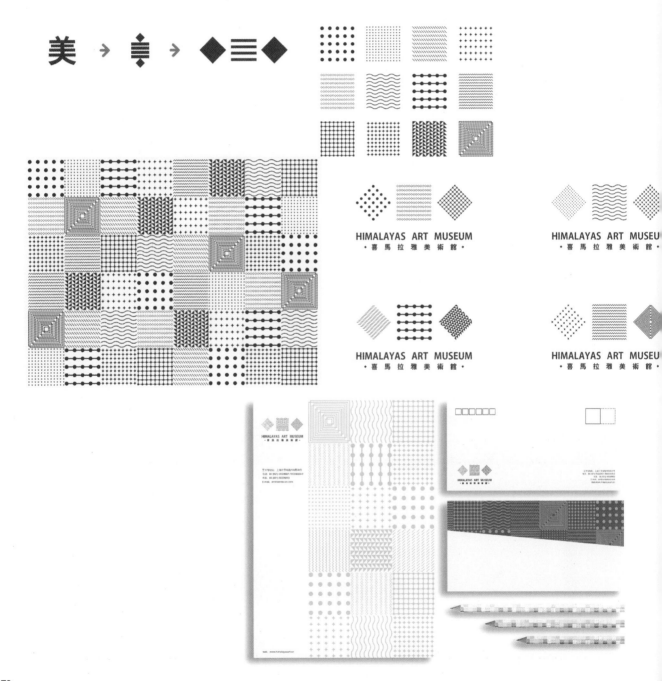

DESIGNER: Li Qi   COUNTRY: China

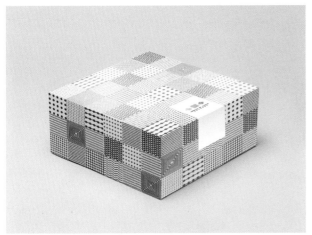

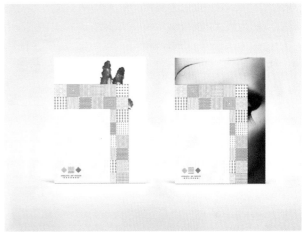

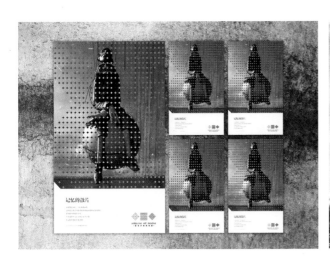

BELLA CENTER

The new identity symbolizes progress, modernity, Danish pride and transport. Transport because it lies in the middle of Copenhagen Airport and Copenhagen city, and those 3 places depend on each other.

Framing

Business

Bella Center

Bella Copenhagen Fashion House

Bella Sky Hotel

Bella International House

Bella Design Center

Copenhagen Congress Center

Part of your brand.

Bella Center

DESIGNER: Thomas Oesterhus   **CLIENT:** Bella Center / Pitch   **COUNTRY:** Norway

Part of your brand.

PRESIDENT

Bella Center

Express your collection

Bella
Copenhagen
Fashion House

CPH FASHION HOUSE 2010

Bella
Copenhagen
Fashion House

Bella
Copenhagen
Fashion House

CPH FASHION HOUSE 2010

Copenhagen Fashion House is Scandinavia's largest fashion house for professionals - a permanent shopping forum at Bella Center where you
as an exhibitor can devote full focus on your
business all year round.

Copenhagen Fashion House is also an integrated
part of Copenhagen International Fashion Fair,
Europe's largest fashion fair, which is held
twice a year.

We believe in the real world, where human re-sources makes a difference.

BC CPH DK EU

Distances:
Malmö - 25 min.
Forum Cph - 15 min.
Cph City - 10 min.
Cph Airport - 10 min.

KUNSTHALLE LUZERN

Corporate Design for the Kunsthalle Luzern. An art museum, gallery in Lucerne Switzerland which is based in the famous Bourbaki Panorama.

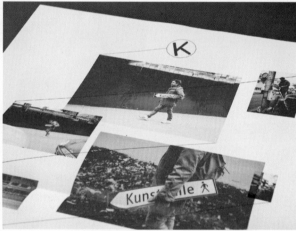

STUDIO: Type Fabric | Atelier für Gestaltung in collaboration with typoundso   **DESIGNER:** Samuel Egloff and Catrina Wipf

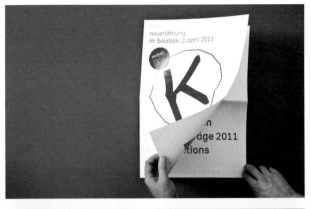

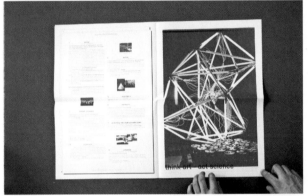

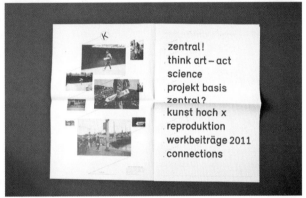

CLIENT: Kunsthalle Luzern   **COUNTRY:** Switzerland

ELEARNING MONTREAL

A unifying event for the online learning industry, eLearning Montreal wanted to develop the industry in Quebec and promote it overseas. Networking concepts and technologies are central to the communication objectives for this visual identity project.

ART DIRECTOR: Marieve Roussel   DESIGNER: Marieve Roussel   CLIENT: Alliance Numérique   COUNTRY: Canada

ORANGE OLIVE

Orange Olive is a promising and challenging startup in the catering business. Orange Olive chooses only pure and honest ingredients for their products. Ingredients that have been manufactured in a respectful manner towards people, animals and our environment.
SILO designed a corporate identity that becomes an illustrated world on its own. Inhabited by fork fish, knife ducks, spoon rabbits, corkscrew woodpeckers and more.

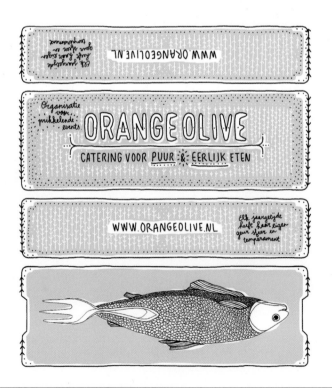

STUDIO: Silo   CREATIVE DIRECTOR: Silo   CLIENT: Orange Olive

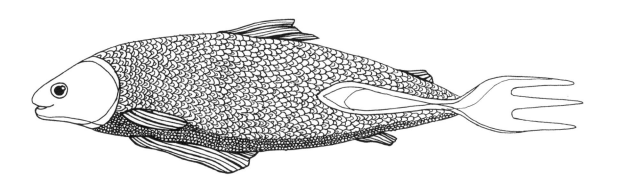

FORKFISH ⌀

COUNTRY: The Netherlands

ORANGEOLIVE

CATERING VOOR _PUUR_ & _EERLIJK_ ETEN

KANKIP KOPKUIKENS   PERCOLATOR~CHICKEN CHICKEN·CUPS

LEPELKONIJN   SPOON RABBIT

VORKVIS   FORKFISH

SPECHTOPENER   CORKSCREW WOODPECKER

·MESEEND·   ·KNIFEDUCK·

~KANDELAARHERT~   ~CHANDELIER DEER~

PERCOLATOR~CHICKEN

SPOON RABBIT

FORKFISH

PERCOLATOR~CHICKEN&CHICKEN·CUPS

SPOON RABBITS

FORKFISH

·KNIFEDUCK·

CORKSCREW WOODPECKER

~CHANDELIER DEER~

KNIFEDUCK

CORKSCREW WOODPECKER

LA LA PLAYLAB LA LA

PLAYLAB

Identity and stationery for Playlab, a workshop space aimed to be a creative playground for stressed adults. The Illustrations are a mixture of scientific elements and random fun images. The stationery is printed in fluorescent Pantone colours while the actual logo is just blind embossed. The address details are filled in using a rubber stamp.

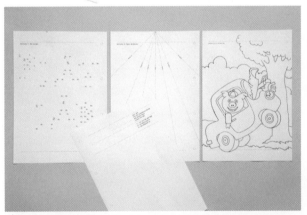

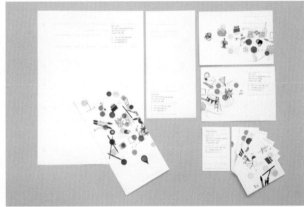

STUDIO: Mind Design   **CREATIVE DIRECTOR:** Holger Jacobs   **CLIENT:** Playlab   **COUNTRY:** UK

SUGARSIN

A distinctly modern sweet shop, SugarSin opens later this year in London. Appointed to design a brand identity, the aim was to communicate the philosophy that sweets are a treat for everybody, not just children.

Having designed a logotype and a playful, lollipop inspired marque & SMITH created an eclectic illustration-led palette for packaging and stationery. Black and white images of everyday objects are combined with accents in primary colours, suggesting a sophisticated tone appealing to adults as well as children.

STUDIO: & SMITH   DESIGNER: & SMITH   CLIENT: Sugarsin   COUNTRY: UK

FRESH
DES
IGN
From Spain
www.spainculture.us

NEW
ARCHI
TECTURE
From Spain
www.spainculture.us

CON
TEMPO
RARY
ART
From Spain
www.spainculture.us

FRESH
DES
IGN
From Spain
www.spainculture.us

NEW
ARCHI
TECTURE
From Spain
www.spainculture.us

CON
TEMPO
RARY
ART
From Spain
www.spainculture.us

SPAIN ARTS & CULTURE

Spain arts & culture is a new brand born to reflect all the expressions of Spain, and convey the cultural variety of the country. The project includes the identity, the stationary and the first program with all the events across the US.

STUDIO: Toormix　　　　CREATIVE DIRECTOR: Ferran mitjans, Oriol armengou　　　　COUNTRY: Spain

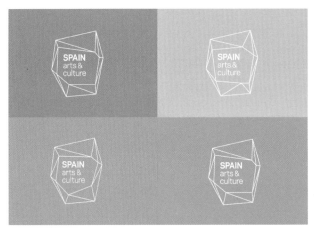

LUX NIJMEGEN

Lux is the largest arthouse cinema in The Netherlands and the cultural engine of the city of Nijmegen. In January 2011 Lux opened a new more exclusive branch called Villa Lux. SILO developed a new brand strategy and visual identity for both Lux and Villa Lux.

STUDIO: Silo   **CREATIVE DIRECTOR:** Silo   **CLIENT:** LUX Nijmegen

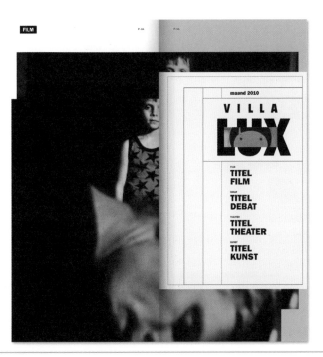

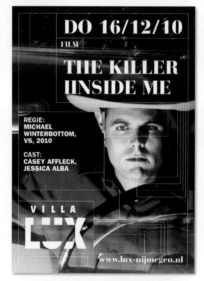

ZA 14/05/11

THEATER

ALLES VOOR DE FÜHRER

Tekst: **Ton Vorstenbosch**
en **Kiek Houthuijsen**
Cast: **wisselende cast van twee acteurs.**

LUX

www.lux-nijmegen.nl

RIBBONESIA

"Ribbonesia" is the art project, which an artist and illustrator 'BAKU' Maeda has been working on. He has always been obsessed in varieties of animals and their expressions and habits since his childhood. His fascination towards animals became his major motif of his daily creation, working with many colors of ribbons and creating various animals. The simple repetition of twisting and bending ribbons sublimes such expressions of animals, capturing the essence of life. Each animal artwork is made by hand with carefully chosen colors, making each one unique. 'BAKU' created the world of Ribbonesia and it is continually expanding.

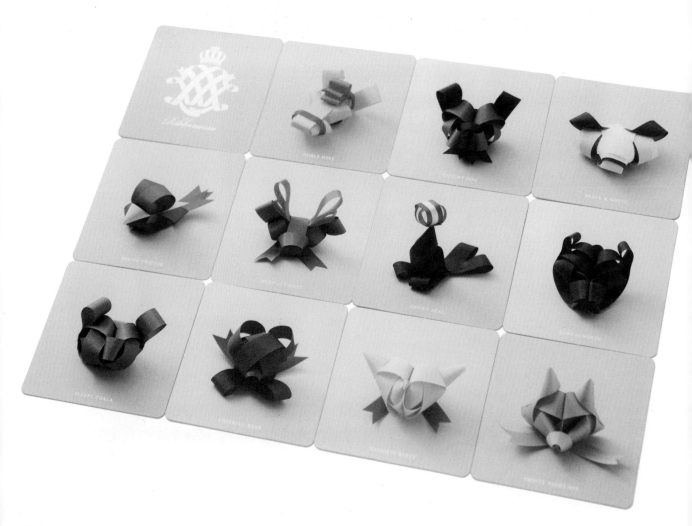

STUDIO: Commune   DESIGNER: Ryo Ueda, Manami Inoue, Daisuke Takada, Yuji Terada   CLIENT: Baku Maeda

COUNTRY: Japan

MAREINER HOLZ

Mareiner Holz has developed a whole range of techniques for finishing untreated wooden boards in an environmentally friendly way. In doing so they discovered that each wood has its own unique character and therefore requires individual techniques in order for its true character to really shine. So much more than just flooring. When "Mareiner Holzindustrie" became simply "Mareiner Holz" it marked not only the adoption of a clear positioning strategy but also the establishment of "Wood Treatment" as a new market category. In addition, an emotional world was created by this courageous brand personality, which is especially evident in the aesthetics of the company's products: 100% natural beauty. As the company's brand mark, Bert the woodpecker is the whimsical representative of the agile outdoorsmen.

STUDIO: moodley brand identity   CREATIVE DIRECTOR: Mike Fuisz   DESIGNER: Wolfgang Niederl

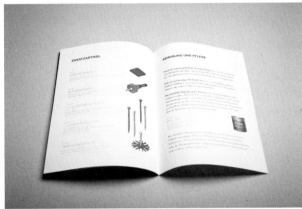

CLIENT: Mareiner Holz　　　　　**COUNTRY:** Austria

NOEEKO ID

The personal brand identity
and some promotional prints
of Noeeko.

STUDIO: Noeeko   DESIGNER: Michal Sycz   CLIENT: Personal

COUNTRY: Poland

°DEICHMANSKE   °DEICHMANSKE   °DEICHMANSKE   °DEICHMANSKE   °DEICHMANSKE   °DEICHMANSKE   °DEICHMANSKE

°DEICHMANSKE   °DEICHMANSKE   °DEICHMANSKE   °DEICHMANSKE   °DEICHMANSKE   °DEICHMANSKE   °DEICHMANSKE

DEICHMANSKE

Branding for the upcoming new Deichmanske Library in Bjorvika, Oslo. The new library is aiming towards becoming one of the most modern and functional libraries in Europe, by combining the old library tradition as well as integrating the new digital media as it evolves further. The identity focuses on the many sides of the institution by building a brand that constantly evolves rather than being static, just as the library itself is supposed to.

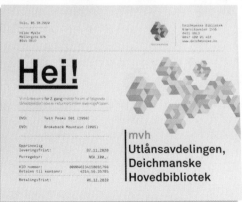

DESIGNER: Mikael Floysand   **CLIENT:** School assignment   **COUNTRY:** Norway

CRISTOVAO CANDEIAS REBRAND

The visual perception and the interpretation of a brand by the audience, it's a fundamental element in a corporative identity.

Convert the letter "C" into a synthesizer and identifying element for the Cristovação Candeias Company, by its graphics and a game concept. The letter "C" comes from the initials of "Cristóvão", "Candeias" and the word "Construction".

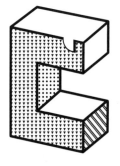

CRISTOVÃO CANDEIAS / INVESTIMENTO IMOBILIÁRIO LDA

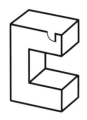

CRISTOVÃO CANDEIAS / INVESTIMENTO IMOBILIÁRIO LDA

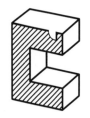

CRISTOVÃO CANDEIAS / INVESTIMENTO IMOBILIÁRIO LDA

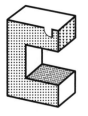

CRISTOVÃO CANDEIAS / INVESTIMENTO IMOBILIÁRIO LDA

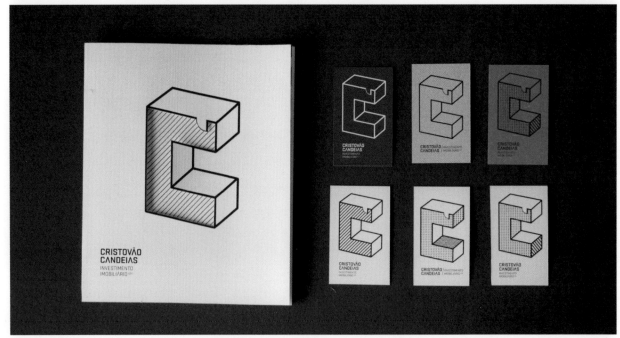

STUDIO: Francisco Elias   **CREATIVE DIRECTOR:** Francisco Elias   **DESIGNER:** Francisco Elias

METEOPHORIC BRAND

Meteophoric Invadder collective is a virtual collective based on Web platforms, created by three young creatives: Francisco Elias, Luís Ribeiro and Rui monteiro. The name results from a set of formal and imagistic definitions, ideas and principles. It is an image that joins an iconic sign, whose referent is the meteorite, with a abstract symbol, metaphor, represented through formal and chromatic effects connoted with the sensation of movement and dynamism. Meteophoric is looking forward to creating a strong impact, similar to that of a meteorite.

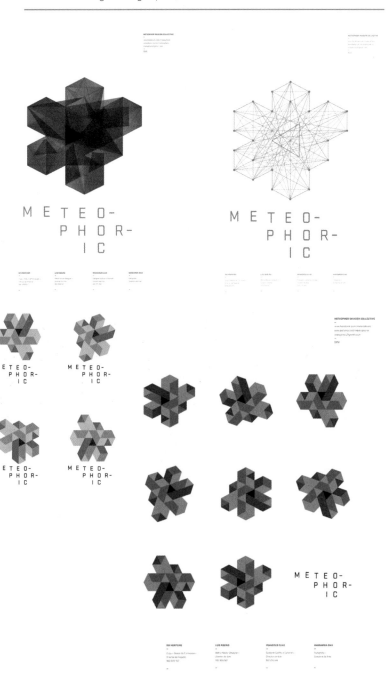

CLIENT: Cristovão Candeias. Investimento imobiliário LDA.
/ Meteophoric Invader Collective   **COUNTRY:** Portugal

CDMA

STUDIO: Viktor Konovalov / Superheroes

DESIGNER: Viktor Konovalov, Yuriy Husinskiy, Andrey Gushin

CLIENT: CDMA Ukraine   **COUNTRY:** Ukraine

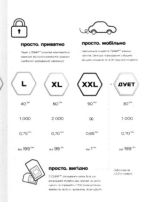

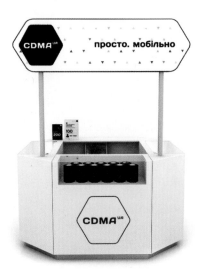

DELTA AWARDS 2011

Visual identity for the Delta Awards 2011, a biannual competition for Industrial Design, organized by ADI-FAD.
A modular system using equilateral triangles which can illustrate any design product. These illustrations identify the various media used for the awards.

STUDIO: Estudio Diego Feijóo   **DESIGNER:** Diego Feijóo   **CLIENT:** ADI-FAD

COUNTRY: Spain

Premis Delta'11

Δ

34a Convocatòria internacional al millor disseny de producte

Premios Delta'11

Δ

34ª Convocatoria internacional al mejor diseño de producto

Delta'11 Awards

Δ

34th International Edition of the Best Product Design

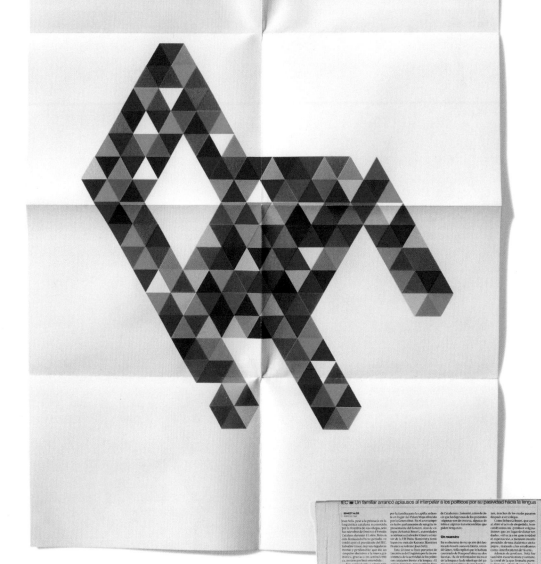

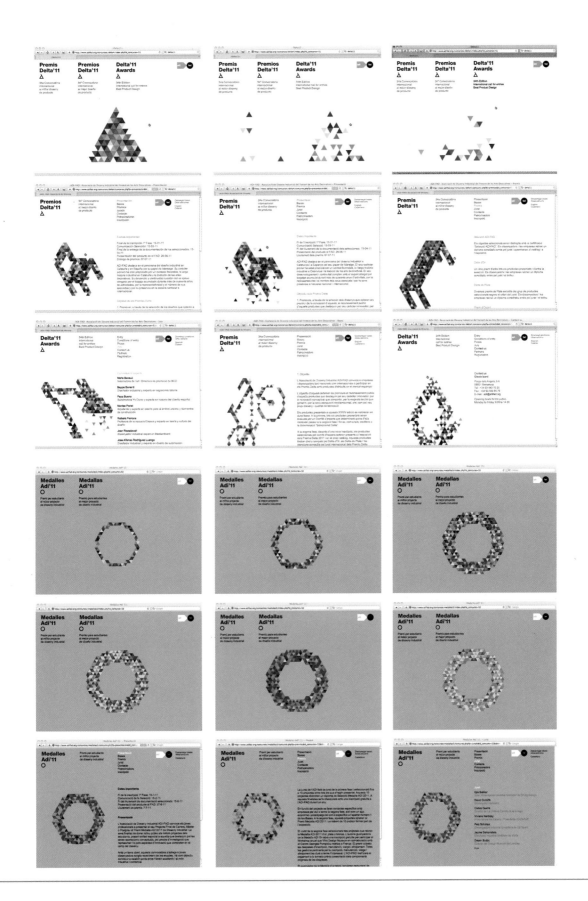

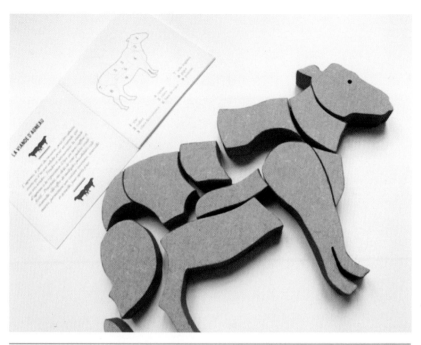

FRIGOS & FILS

Identity, posters, flyers, packaging, leaflet, press kit, website of "Frigos & Fils", a new store, school and restaurant dedicated to the meat.
Les Frigos de Paris is an amazing place lost in a really modern district in Paris. It was an ancient refrigerated station where we stocked food (particularly meat).
Elsa was inspired by the history of the place and wanted to make something which really contrast with the industrial area.
So she imagine a place dedicated to the meat, where you can buy it, cook it, eat it, and learn how to cut it, as a butcher shop, restaurant, and butcher school.

DESIGNER: Elsa ANTOINE   **CLIENT:** School project   **COUNTRY:** UK

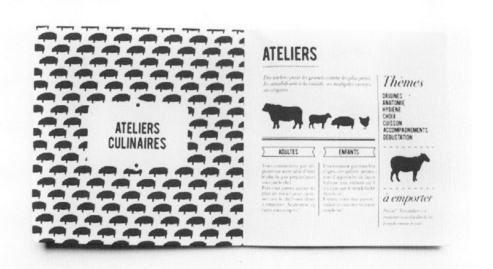

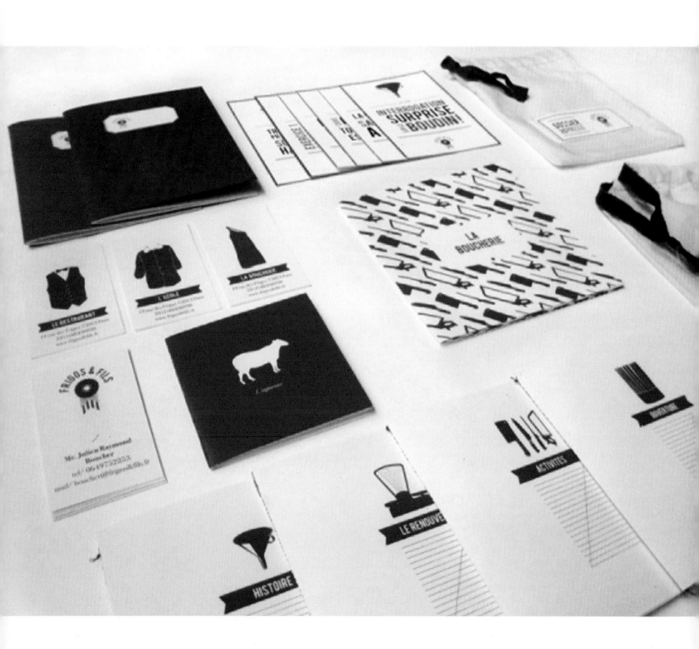

JACK OF ALL TRADES

The whole corporate identity for the Skate & Aparel Store.
"Jack of all Trades" was designed based on the certain
"sense of an old neighborhood shop", where you can find
anything from watches to shoes, inspired by its name "Jack
of all Trades".

STUDIO: Zazdesign graphic lab   DESIGNER: Daria, Zinaida Zazirei   CLIENT: Dimitrios Tsevas

TRULY DEEPLY

Truly Deeply is the re-branding of Storm Design and Brand DNA. The illustrations and designs were created to express the brand essence 'Re-imaging Brands'. The delivery is magical and thoughtful. The sliced animals represent a new way of thinking about brand to create new and unique brands to take to market.

STUDIO: Truly Deeply   **CREATIVE DIRECTOR:** David Ansett   **DESIGNER:** David Ansett, Derek Carroll, Cassandra Gill, Tim Wood, Lachlan McDougall

CLIENT: Truly Deeply   COUNTRY: Australia

SPUDBAR

Spudbar is a retail franchise offering the best baked potato in the country. Truly Deeply used the wholesome personality of the humble potato to create a strong sense of localism and down-to-earth nature. Building a strong visual style that was wholesome and comfortable was the key to creating a retail experience that could be enjoyed by all. The visuals that were created formed the design suite for all collateral and were applied to a range of corporate and marketing materials.

STUDIO: Truly Deeply   **CREATIVE DIRECTOR:** David Ansett   **DESIGNER:** Cassandra Gill, Lachlan McDougall

Antony Morell
Director
antony.morell@spudbar.com.au
Spudbar
Suite1, 574 Plummer St
Port Melbourne VIC 3207
M. 0402 251 428
P. 03 8638 9999
F. 03 9646 5455
www.spudbar.com.au

Antony Morell
Director
antony.morell@spudbar.com.au
Spudbar
Suite1, 574 Plummer St
Port Melbourne VIC 3207
M. 0402 251 428
P. 03 8638 9999
F. 03 9646 5455
www.spudbar.com.au

richmond@spudbar.com.au
226 Swan Street
Richmond VIC
P. +61 3 9421 6033
F. +61 3 9421 6066
www.spudbar.com.au

Trish
Manager
richmond@spudbar.com.au
226 Swan Street
Richmond VIC
P. +61 3 9421 6033
F. +61 3 9421 6066
www.spudbar.com.au

CLIENT: Spudbar   COUNTRY: Australia

chocolate

CHOCHOCO

Chochoco is a shop selling chocolate. The logo used flowing lines to represent the richness of the chocolate. The color of black and golden reflects modernity and elegance while adding powder blue and pink to get close to the consumers and highlighting the dreamlike feeling of the chocolate. The custom illustration seems like a magic and delivers the brand spirit of chochoco.

STUDIO: 2TIGERS design studio   DESIGNER: Kuan Yu, Gina, Xie BingFang, Lin LingJun   CLIENT: Chochoco chocolate

REGION: Taiwan (P.R.C)

GELATI SKY

Gelati Sky started as a boutique which ranges from servicing restaurants and specialist food shops. The packaging was the strongest step to building a brand that consumers could connect with. As a small ultra premium brand, the package needed to take on a more delicate personality than the bigger, more established companies. The taste of the Gelati is simply amazing and if it was a rich, beautiful label, one that would get buyers and customers excited, it would be very successful.

STUDIO: Truly Deeply   **CREATIVE DIRECTOR:** David Ansett   **DESIGNER:** Cassandra Gill, Lachlan McDougall

CLIENT: Gelati Sky   **COUNTRY:** Australia

MAK

MAK - Moscow Communication Academy, the new generation/way educational institution, which graduates new staff for communicational industry. The Academy combines with university, creative studio, master classes and professional community.

14.07–18.07
Летний интенсив
«Hot Workshop»

МОСКОВСКАЯ
АКАДЕМИЯ
КОММУНИКАЦИЙ

DESIGNER: Pitertsev Mikhail   **CLIENT:** Bhsad   **COUNTRY:** Russia

RESTAURANT HINDENBURG

Restaurant Hindenburg - is created like a prewar art deco with atmosphere airship building.

Hindenburg brochure - is issued by Ginderdur restaurant quarterly. It's dedicated to remarkable events of the past and present of airship building. The main aim of the brochure is to entertain and educate the visitors of the restaurant.

DESIGNER: Pitertsev Mikhail   **CLIENT:** Restaurant Hindenburg   **COUNTRY:** Russia

NEOLAB

Neolab is an IT company specialising in building and connecting business information systems, web applications and websites.

Because Neolab creates and connects new web environments, IlovarStritar designed their corporate identity to imitate an open, developing ecosystem. Various motifs that form the logo together with the Neolab text. Motifs were selected based on their meaning, such as images of a pigeon and a cheetah for the envelope (postal service + speed).

STUDIO: IlovarStritar   CREATIVE DIRECTOR: Robert Ilovar   DESIGNER: Robert Ilovar

LET'S DO THE
YIGLOO

1 PICK A CUP 2 MIX ANY FLAVOR 3 DRESS ME UP 4 ENJOY YUM!

YIGLOO

Yigloo Yogurt is all about fun and happiness. It is to appeal to kids as well as adults in a pretty broad sense.

How and where these characters are placed is rather intentional so that they interact with the real environment - which is almost all white-out. Refurbished and recycled furniture were whitewashed and re-used in the space to also underline the owners' support for the eco-friendly and green movement.

STUDIO: Foreign Policy Design Group   CREATIVE DIRECTOR: Yah-Leng Yu   DESIGNER: Cheryl Chong, Yah-Leng Yu

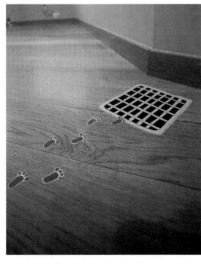

CLIENT: Yigloo Yogurt   COUNTRY: Singapore

THE WATERHOUSE AT SOUTH BUND

The brand identity is based on the concept of DUALITY. Shanghai has a DUALITY persona in almost every aspect of its DNA. Hence an 'IN & OUT', 'BLACK & WHITE', reversible concept - aptly reflects the architectural design intent of inside out, outside in.

STUDIO: Foreign Policy Design Group   CREATIVE DIRECTOR: Yah-Leng Yu, Arthur Chin

DESIGNER: Tianyu Isaiah Zheng (TY), Yah-Leng Yu   **CLIENT:** The Waterhouse at South Bund   **COUNTRY:** Singapore

APOTEK HJARTAT

Graphic identity as well as applications e.g. façade signs, bags, navigation systems, images, campaign communication, website design, printed material for customer loyalty club, information brochures, profile programme for office printed matter, participation at development of new shop concept.

The aim was to create a logo that could win the hearts of the Swedish people. The greatest challenge was to find a balance between knowledge and credibility on one hand, and cordiality and service on the other. The traffic-light green colour is an obvious signal that is easy to see and identify. The iconic heart symbol is unique because of its opening in the centre, which creates a feeling of openness and welcome.

STUDIO: Bvd   **CREATIVE DIRECTOR:** Susanna Nygren Barrett   **DESIGNER:** Rikard Ahlberg, Bengt Anderung, Andreas Helin, Tom Eriksson, Karin Sundberg

APOTEK♡

Ont i huvudet

Ont i huvudet
De flesta människor har ont i huvudet ibland. Det finns många olika slags huvudvärk, och många olika anledningar till att den uppstår.
Här får du några tips om vart du kan göra, hur Apotek Hjärtat kan hjälpa dig, och när det är bäst att gå till vårdcentral eller läkare.

Spänningshuvudvärk
Spänningshuvudvärk känns ofta som en tryckande eller molande värk, eller "som att ha ett band runt huvudet".
Värken kommer ofta i perioder på några timmar, eller någon dag. Det finns också ett fåtal människor som har kronisk spänningshuvudvärk, och alltså har ont jämt.

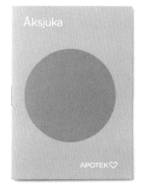

Åksjuka

Akut-p-piller

Ont i stjärten och mask

Gaser i magen

Allergi i näsan och ögonen

CLIENT: Apotek Hjartat   **COUNTRY**: Sweden

TYPE TRUMPS

Type Trumps, a play on Top Trumps, is a game in which different typefaces are attributed numerical values. These figures are then used to enable the cards to be won or lost using some of the tried and tested 'Top Trumps' rules. The Type Trumps has a 'ranking', which is a subjectively ascribed positional value based on my personal favorites.

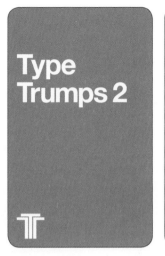

STUDIO: Face37   CREATIVE DIRECTOR: Rick Banks   DESIGNER: Rick Banks

Tephra 0
Weights 6
Price £351
Tephra 12
Legibility 5
Cuts 1
Tephra 50
Date 2007
Rank 17
Tephra 100
Designer
Hamish Muir
Tephra 136
Special Power
8vo

Typeface easyscriptweigh tsthreepriceone hundredthirty fourspecialpowe rbgsixyeartw othousandtwocu tsonelegibilityf iverankthirtee ndesignerjoelno rdströmfoundry lineto

CBS DIDOT FOUNDRY DAYLIGHT PRICE NA YEAR NINETEEN SIXTY SIX CUTS ONE LEGIBILITY SEVEN WEIGHTS ONE RANK TWELVE SPECIAL POWER LOU DORFSMAN DESIGNER FREEMAN CRAW

KNOCKOUT

**H&FJ, 611 BROADWAY, NEW YORK
MONDAY NIGHT, DECEMBER 1994**

BOTH WEIGHING IN AT 32, SPECIAL POWERS...

—

JONATHAN
HOEFLER

vs

TOBIAS
FRERE-JONES

**ADMISSION PRICES — $499.00
RANK 11 LEGIBILITY 07 CUTS 01**

Weights 12
Rank 3
Year 2009
Legibility 08
Cuts 1
Special Power
Foundry
British Trains
A2—TYPE
Designer
Margaret Calvert
Jock Kinneir &
Henrik Kubel

On Pay Trains please state your destination to the Guard and tender the exact fare if possible. Check that your ticket shows the correct date and fair paid, retaining it for examination or collection.

New Rail Alphabet
Price £1000.

typeface archive catalogue solid. weights 02. rank 06. special power 02. cuts 02. designer 1970. legibility. price 775. pounds. year 06. lineto the foundry.

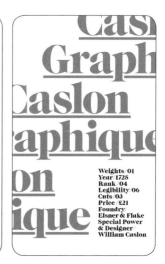

Caslon Graph Caslon aphique on ique

Weights / 01
Year / 1725
Rank / 04
Legibility / 06
Cuts / 03
Price / £21
Foundry / Elsner & Flake
Special Power / & Designer / William Caslon

Bodoni is a series† of serif typefaces first designed by *Giambattista Bodoni* (1740—1813) in c1798. The typeface is classified as didone modern.

Bauer Bodoni (£133) from *Adobe* has eight weights, a legibility of six and a ranking of one. Bodoni has many special powers‡.

‡ 86 cuts
† *Massimo Vignelli*

Typeface FF Johannes G. Foundry FontFont. Price 35 pounds. Year 1450 — 1455 Euro 01. Rank 28. Legibility 02. Weights 01. Special Power The Printing Press. Designer Johannes Gensfleisch zur Laden zum Gutenberg (c. 1398 – February 3, 1468) was a German goldsmith and printer who is credited with being the first European to use movable type printing, in around 1439, and the global inventor of the mechanical printing press. His major work, the Gutenberg Bible (also known as the 42-line Bible), has been acclaimed for its high aesthetic and technical quality. Among the specific contributions to printing that are attributed to Gutenberg are the invention of a process for mass-producing movable type, the use of oil-based ink, and the use of a wooden printing press similar to the screw olive and wine presses of the period. His truly epochal invention was the combination of these elements into a practical system. been familiar with printing; it is claimed that he had worked on copper engravings with an artist known as the Master of the Playing Cards. One Gutenberg method for producing type is traditionally considered to have included a type metal alloy and a hand mould for casting type. The use of movable type was a marked improvement on the handwritten manuscript, which was the existing method of book manufacturing in Europe, and up on woodblock printing, and revolutionized European book-making. Gutenberg's printing technology spread rapidly throughout Europe and is considered a key factor in the European Renaissance. Gutenberg remains a towering figure in the popular image; in 1999, the Rank'd Network ranked Gutenberg number one on their People of the Millennium countdown, and in 1999, Time–Life magazine picked Gutenberg's invention as the most important of the second millennium.

BEANS
PRICE £89
YEAR 2008
CUTS 04
RANK 49
WEIGHTS 04
LEGIBILITY 02
DESIGNERS CHARLES GRANT DIETER ZEMBSCH
FOUNDRY LINETO
SPECIAL POWER MICHAEL C. PLACE

CLIENT: Face37   **COUNTRY:** UK

EGOSOUND

Total identity for egosound, a new company created out of two existing companies namely Ego and Soundboard. Both companies coach artists on a personal, financial and creative level.

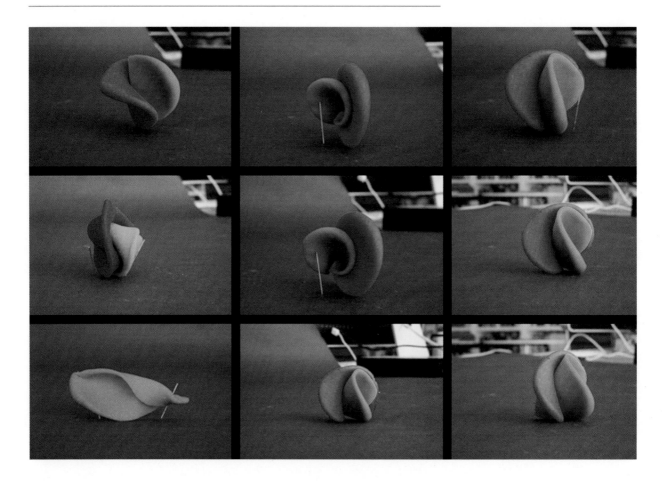

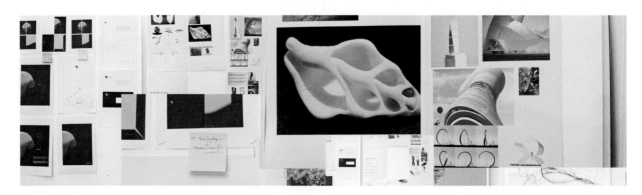

STUDIO: Coming Soon   CREATIVE DIRECTOR: Jim Van Raemdonck   DESIGNER: Alexander Popelier

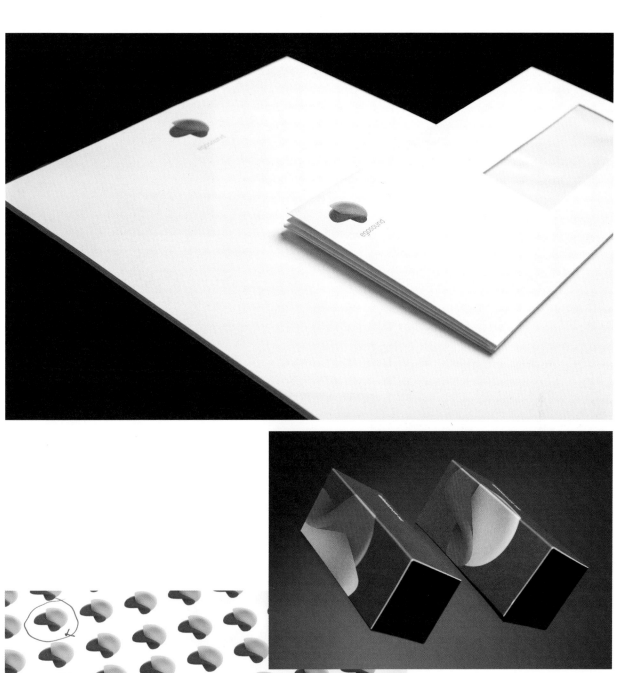

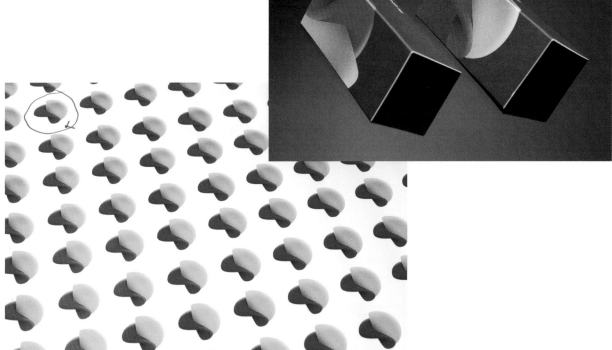

CLIENT: Egosound   COUNTRY: Belgium

STUDIO: Ivan Khmelevsky   DESIGNER: Ivan Khmelevsky   CLIENT: Lion Is The Sun Promo Agency

LION IS THE SUN

Lion Is The Sun is the best agency in Moscow when it comes to contemporary music. It has organized show for many artists including Doom, Fucked Up, Japandroids, Themselves, No Age and many more.

Besides stationary, Ivan also designed badges, stickers, T-shirts and tote bags for people to support the independent promo agencies and to show that they share the same values as the promoters.

THE STORY UNFOLDS

The Story Unfolds (TSU) is a retail concept that allows creatives and designers alike to publish their own books and sell them right at the store. With a wide selection of both self-published titles as well as books by established authors, TSU gives a sense of prestige to independent authors in how they sell and distribute their creative books. All self-published titles will be given the same treatment as their established counterparts in how they are displayed, packaged, marketed and sold at the store.

The concept of an unfolding origami is used as an analogy to tell the story behind the concept. All of us have a story to tell. It could be a story about our drawings or a story about our photos, or an actual story for a novel. TSU helps unfold them.

STUDIO: The Launch Room   **DESIGNER:** Leong Huang Zi   **CLIENT:** TSU Marketplace

COUNTRY: Malaysia

JOHANNA LENANDER

Johanna Lenander is a Writer & Editor, living and working in New York City. She needed a site that not only displayed her writing skills but also reflected her sense of style. Lundgren+Lindqvist were approached to design and build the site and to design Johanna Lenander's identity and printed matter.

The site would give the visitor a quick overview enabling them to assess the information of interest rapidly. The aesthetic, both of the identity and website, follows the editorial tradition of classic newspapers, but with a modern twist. They used the WordPress CMS as a platform for the site which enables Johanna to easily edit the site and upload new work. Printing techniques include relief and fluorescent inks and high quality paper stock such as the uncoated Munken Polar 400gsm was used for the stationery.

 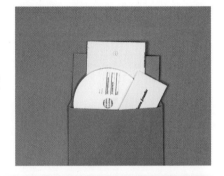

STUDIO: Lundgren+Lindqvist **CREATIVE DIRECTOR:** Andreas Friberg Lundgren **CLIENT:** Johanna Lenander **COUNTRY:** Sweden
Carl-Johan Lindqvist

ESTIVO

Estivo's main target is women of every size, color and shape that are tired of the artificial approach of the female media. Taking this as the main concept, Wallnut Studio developed the whole visual strategy based on fruits: natural, fresh, beautiful and diverse.

STUDIO: Wallnut Studio   **DESIGNER:** Cristina Londoño   **CLIENT:** Estivo   **COUNTRY:** Colombia

RESTAURANT MAAEMO

Maaemo is an ecological gourmet restaurant in Oslo, Norway. The restaurant has a Norwegian owner, Danish cook and a Finnish sommelier, so it is truly a Scandinavian collaboration. The cuisine of Maaemo is Nordic, and the name and colour scheme derive from Finnish, meaning "Mother Earth".

The design for Maaemo is inspired by Scandinavian nature and architecture, reflected in the lines, shapes, rhythm and light creating a poetic, Nordic modernism. It gives the restaurant its atmosphere with consistent use of shape and color, incorporating features such as the chair, a Danish design classic, the askew pendulum lamp, and the overall design, both interior and exterior.

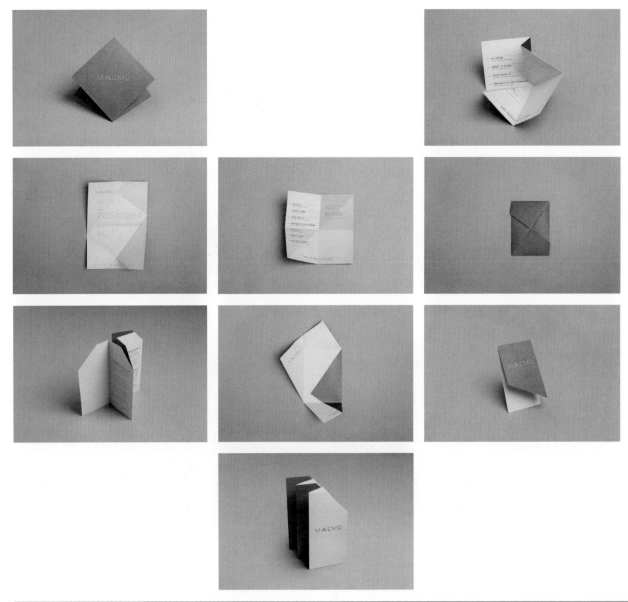

STUDIO: Uniform Strategic Design   **DESIGNER**: Ludvig Bruneau Rossow, Torgeir Hjetland   **CLIENT**: Restaurant Maaemo

COUNTRY: Norway

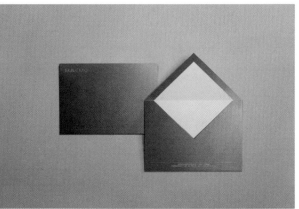

PREVIEW SPAIN

Graphic design for different cultural programs organized by the Spanish Embassy in Washington DC. The graphic concept for the 2008 program was a contemporary vision of the "mantilla" (a traditional Spanish piece of textile), the 2009 edition was the famous "paella" and the 2010 was a graphic play with the Spanish European presidency. All these programs carried a poster inside and also some related objects as souvenirs.

STUDIO: Toormix   CREATIVE DIRECTOR: Ferran mitjans, Oriol armengou   COUNTRY: Spain

PICCOLINA

Piccolina is a Scandinavian antique shop that offers a variety of collectibles. One of the reasons why antiques are so appealing is that they preserve an aspect of the values or culture from people living in a different period. Each antique item tells customers something about Scandinavian history or culture. 14 different Scandinavian icons are used to form the shop logo, which could be used on a range of promotional tools, such as wrapping paper, direct mailings and Sapporo shop signage. Each of the icons is important history and it can all be found at Piccolina.

piccolina
from Scandinavia

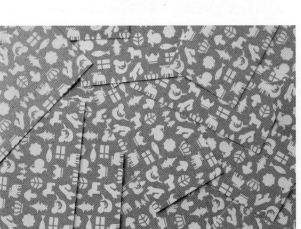

STUDIO: Commune   **DESIGNER:** Ryo Ueda, Manami Inoue, Daisuke Takada, Yuji Terada   **CLIENT:** Piccolina

COUNTRY: Japan

MARAWA THE AMAZING

Identity for Marawa (The Amazing), an internationally well-known Hula Hoop artist and performer. The logo is based on Revue theatre display fonts which often use lightbulbs. The stationery is printed in many variations using 3 Pantone colours and black and white images.

STUDIO: Mind Design   **CREATIVE DIRECTOR:** Holger Jacobs   **DESIGNER:** Romilly Winter, Sara Streule

CLIENT: Marawa The Amazing   **COUNTRY:** UK

GXY SEARCH

From sport to fashion, lifestyle to advertising, GXY's clients all offer 'excitement jobs' – the type of jobs many Gen X&Yers dream about. One of the defining attributes of Gen X&Y is they see themselves as distinct individuals who belong to a range of overlapping tribes. The brand identity for GXY was a reflection of their own status within the Gen X&Y tribes they belong to. The brand identity concept was developed through Truly Deeply creative brand design process and was applied to business stationery, signage and website.

GXY SEARCH

STUDIO: Truly Deeply   **CREATIVE DIRECTOR:** David Ansett   **DESIGNER:** Lachlan McDougall

CLIENT: GXY Search   **COUNTRY:** Australia

CRD

The Aulnay-sous-Bois Conservatory of Music and Dance (usually called CRD) trains prospective artists. It is also a place for research and musical creation. The Conservatory offers concerts and performances all year round. Identity and logo reflect rythm, vibration and sound.

Retchka designs graphic and musical logos composed of mathematical and geometric shapes in which colour plays a musical role, using both solid colours and shaded tones.

The studio has also created a special typeface by adding dots on several letters, so that the text looks like a musical score.

The CRD's identity appears on different documents : quarterly programs, monthly posters, letterheads, signage.

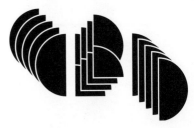

CONSERVATOIRE
DE MUSIQUE ET DE DANSE
À RAYONNEMENT DÉPARTEMENTAL
AULNAY-SOUS-BOIS

STUDIO: www.retchka.fr   **DESIGNER:** Nelly Schwartz, Sylvain Guily   **CLIENT:** Ville d'Aulnay-sous-Bois

SAISON MUSICALE
DU CONSERVATOIRE

Le programme musical est disponible dans toutes
les structures municipales.

OCT.
NOV.
DEC.
20'10

CONSERVATOIRE
DE MUSIQUE ET DE DANSE
À RAYONNEMENT DÉPARTEMENTAL
AULNAY-SOUS-BOIS

PROGRAMME MUSICAL
DU CONSERVATOIRE

JAN.
FEV.
MARS.
20'11

CONSERVATOIRE
DE MUSIQUE ET DE DANSE
À RAYONNEMENT DÉPARTEMENTAL
AULNAY-SOUS-BOIS

COUNTRY: France

DESEO

Deseo biscuit line contains:
Breakfast biscuits (gold packets)
Cantucci and butter biscuits in PVC packets
Cantucci and butter biscuits in boxes (for luxury food shops)
Gift boxes (steel box)
Olive Oil biscuits (boxes with "oil drop seal")
Aperitif salted biscuits (black packets)

STUDIO: Doni & Associati   **DESIGNER:** Simonetta Doni, Giuliano Fenn   **CLIENT:** Deseo Srl

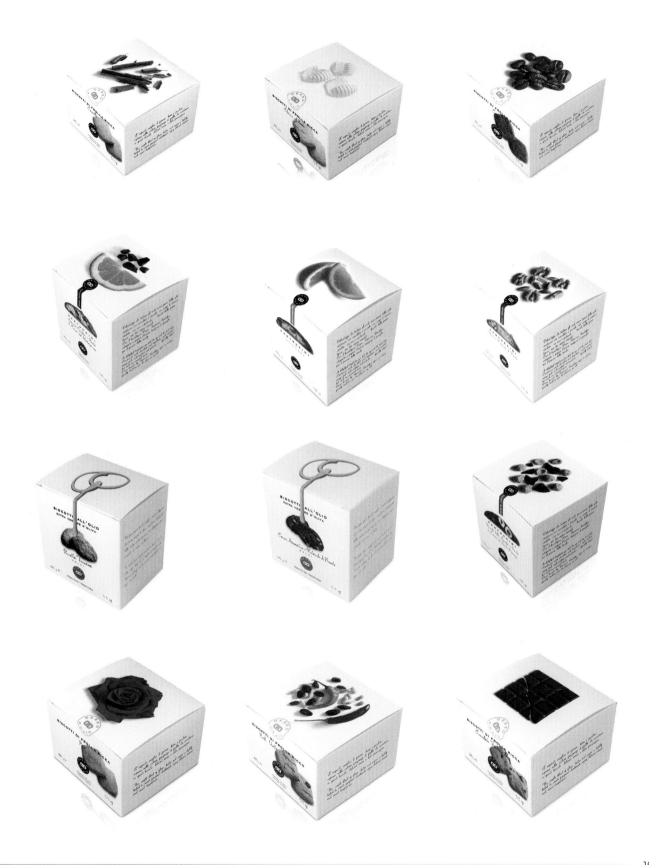

UTRECHT CITY THEATRE

The keywords in the programme at Utrecht City Theatre are excitement and reflection. The interaction between visitors and performers is an exciting and emotional adventure, also leading to reflective moments. Every meeting is the start of something new. This is symbolised by the logo. The typography and colour composition reflect the zeitgeist of Dudok, architect of the theatre building. The edgy play of letters places the City Theatre self-consciously and challengingly in the here and now.

STUDIO: Edenspiekermann   **CREATIVE DIRECTOR:** Edo van Dijk   **DESIGNER:** Hannah Manneke, Arjan van Zeumeren, Jan Dirk Porsius

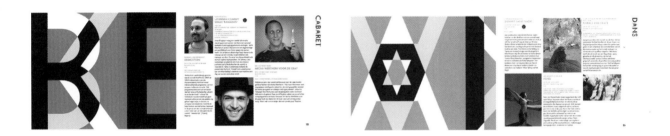

CLIENT: Stadsschouwburg Utrecht   **COUNTRY:** The Netherlands

G-DAY DESIGN

This is a brand identity of a graphic design studio whose English name is G-day with the meaning of period in Chinese. The creative element is dots which mean idea, concept and inspiration in Chinese. An unlimited creative space and interactive function are created among three dots, which are good at raising new directions and concepts.

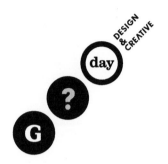

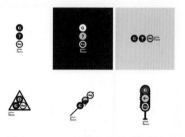

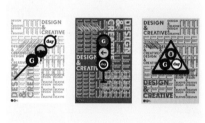

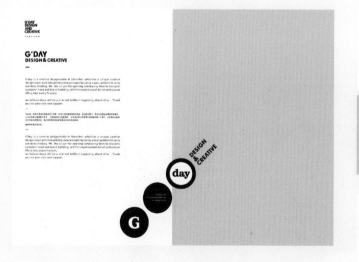

STUDIO: G-day Studio   **DESIGNER:** Chen JiaSheng   **CLIENT:** G-day Studio   **COUNTRY:** China

A-5

A-5 is a dynamic youth program for towns in the Region of Murcia (Spain) with less than five thousand inhabitants.

The purpose of this project is to create a general brand for the program and one brand for each of those nine municipalities.

Ojós

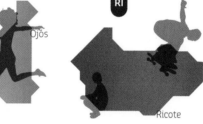
Ricote

Ulea

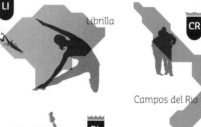
Librilla

Villanueva del Segura

Campos del Rio

Pliego

Aledo

Albudeite

DESIGNER: Romualdo Faura   **CLIENT:** Instituto de la Juventud de la Region de Murcia   **COUNTRY:** Spain

169

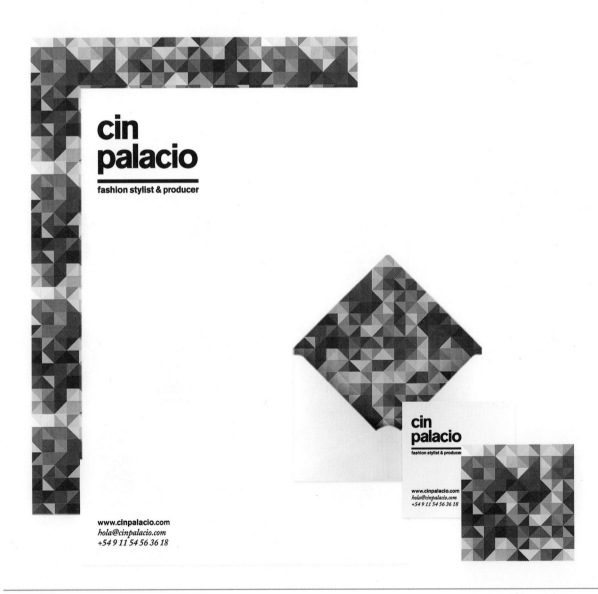

STUDIO: Pogo

ADVANCE NONWOVEN

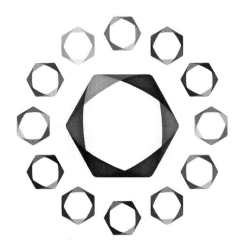

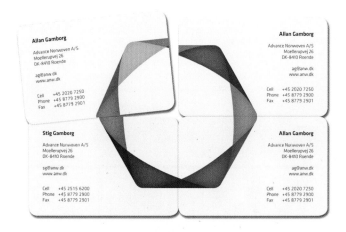

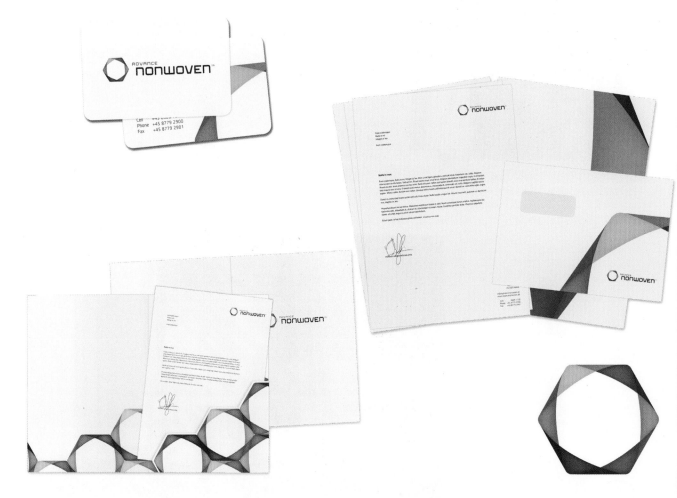

STUDIO: ME! ME! ME!　　　　　**DESIGNER**: Tom Nielsen, Mads Katholm, Christian Hansen　　　　　**COUNTRY**: Denmark

HOTEL AMBROSE

Ambrose is a little hotel in Montreal. The hotel occupies two Victorian style buildings, built in 1910. The logotype is classic like Victorian style but fresh.

STUDIO: Imprvd with kissmiklos   **DESIGNER:** Miklos Kiss   **CLIENT:** Hotel Ambrose   **COUNTRY:** Hungary

LACK MAGAZINE

LACK magazine is a new Hungarian fashion magazine.

New Hungarian fashion magazine cover design and cover bag idea and insight design, graphic design, and typography. Miklos wanted to design a new progressive cover concept. Miklos observed many times how the women hold the magazines in their hands and how often they get in inconvenient situations because they can't hold the magazines in a more comfortable way. Furthermore, Miklos noticed that moving people potentially represent the best commercial. This was the base of the idea to create a cover which resembles a handbag. Women walk with it around more easily and it works like a live commercial. The cover does not only resemble a handbag by its shape, but also, every further issue will appear with a cloth sample, so the material would look similar too.

STUDIO: Kissmiklos   CREATIVE DIRECTOR: Miklos Kiss   DESIGNER: Miklos Kiss

CLIENT: LACK magazine   **COUNTRY:** Hungary

RETRO MOJOCOFFEE

Retro mojocoffee is the second café of mojocoffee. The interior of it continues the Northern European style from the first store which is charactered by the square book shelf linking with the first floor and the double desk. Therefore, 2TIGER use the concept of lattice as the main element in the retro mojocoffee, such as card, menu, cup mat, graphics and exterior of the café.

retr○

STUDIO: 2TIGERS design studio   DESIGNER: Yu DaiGuan, Lin LingJun   CLIENT: Retro Mojocoffee

REGION: Taiwan (P.R.C)

SOFT!

Soft!™ sells softserve icecream. White is chosen as the base colour, which is also the colour of the vanilla ice-cream they use. A quirky tagline and colourful illustrations give the brand a fun image.

STUDIO: Bravo Company   **CLIENT:** Omnigio Pacific   **COUNTRY:** Singapore

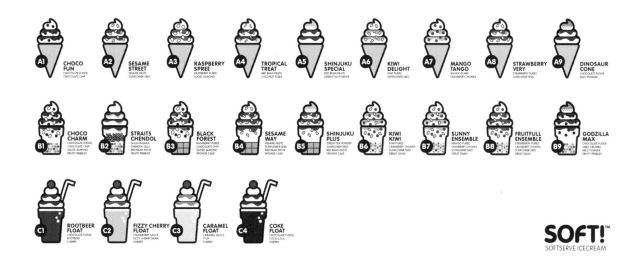

SOFT!™
SOFTSERVE ICECREAM

GABBANI

STUDIO: Demian

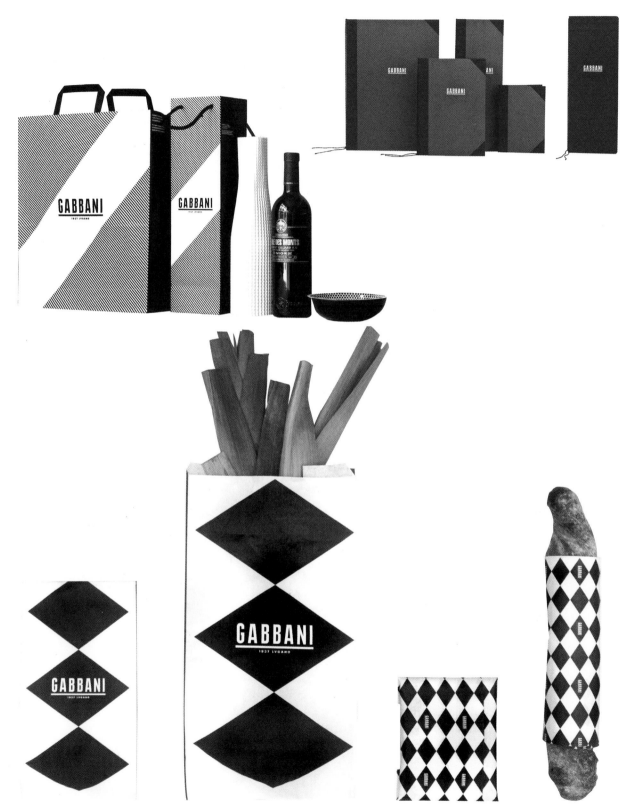

ANTONIONI DVD BOX

This Project was created on the occasion of the 15th anniversary of the Gutek Film Company. The Gutek film company deals with the promotion and distribution of the world cinematography. This collection is a special, collector's edition of the 8 films, the classics of an artistic Italian cinematography of Michelangelo Antonioni. The target of the product is a specific, not accidental audience but the film art lovers. The film art is multi-leveled, sophisticated and a little difficult to perceive. The form of package refers to these film art notions by making the user to put some effort into proceeding a range of actions allowing him to get the reach of the content of the box.

DESIGNER: Rajmund Rajchel   **CLIENT:** Gutek Film   **COUNTRY:** Poland

RAFF / BENETTON

RAFF is a Norwegian design event focusing on design, textile and fashion made by people from the city of Bergen. Oh Yeah Studio was lucky enough to be a part of this as Hans is from the west coast and we both have Bergen in their hearts after living and working there a while ago.

So, both young and established designers from the region had their own exhibition in selected stores around the city, lasting a full week. At Benetton they got two nice and big windows to show off our work. They called the project 'Oh Yeah Bergen' as it was a great opportunity to promote Oh Yeah studio in Bergen. In the visuals we incorporated drops of water (it rains a lot in Bergen), which we printed onto t-shirts, singlets, bags, screen-printed posters and also on a smaller bag to use as a gift bag for the products.

STUDIO: Oh Yeah Studio   **DESIGNER:** Hans Christian Øren, Christina Magnussen   **CLIENT:** Raff Bergen

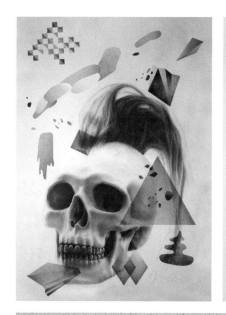

THE BEAUTIFUL PEEPHOLE

The Beautiful Peephole is the 2nd part of my Resn-fy style exploration.
I was inspired and motivated by the works of Resn. I siphoned what
I have grasped and blended them into my works. I created a hollow
looking sphere to represent a peephole and filled it up with elements
that will constitute bold and raw. Bony and cartilaginous framework is
to symbolize the termination of life. Death could be a comprehensive
subject, it can be beautiful. Beauty is what inspires emotion rather
than intellectual appreciation.

THE PLAYGIRL

The Playgirl is a commissioned work I have done for Digital Arts
UK magazine. I walk the readers through some of Photoshop CS5
latest features. Besides that, I show the readers how you can take
transformation and composition to a whole new level.

CREATIVE DIRECTOR: Ee Venn Soh   DESIGNER: Ee Venn Soh   CLIENT: Personal

YAW

YAW / YOU ARE WE. It is a magazine by The Keystone Design Union dedicated to uncovering what makes the creative mind tick. It is a conversation from the cutting edge. I am tasked to create my interpretation of YAW in a typographic manner.

SPRING FEVER

Spring Fever is an artwork created for the Desktopography exhibition. I am creating a feeling of restlessness, excitement and laziness brought on by the coming of spring. It is full of energy and vitality.

THE DINO CLUB

The Dino Club is the 1st part of my Resn-fy style exploration. I was inspired and motivated by the works of Resn. I siphoned what I have grasped and blended them into my works. I fabricated a relic of the past by getting in dinosaurs in traditional drawings. Later, I bring in various fruits and blend them into one mass. The whole purpose is to create a primitive state of existence, untouched and uninfluenced by civilization.

COUNTRY: Malaysia

C'EST OUVERT

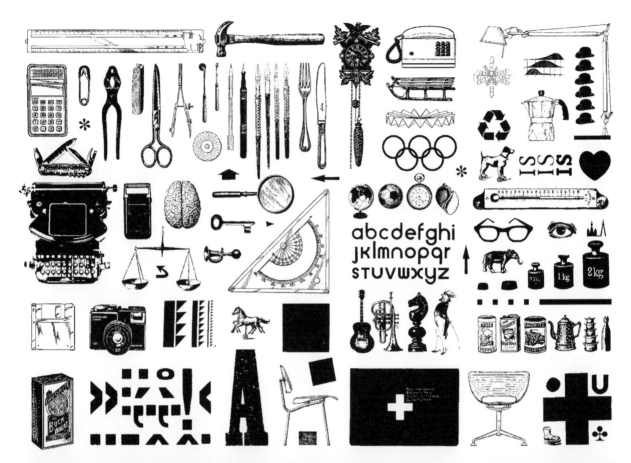

STUDIO: Demian

BOMBAYSAPPHIRE

Bacardi Norway and Bleed are cooperating to host the prestigious Bombay Sapphire Designer Glass Competition on a national level for the first time in three years. The challenge, aimed primarily at students, is to create a new, innovative design for the classic Martini glass. Bleed launched the competition with two shiny posters, six different flyers and a sweet little intro for the website.

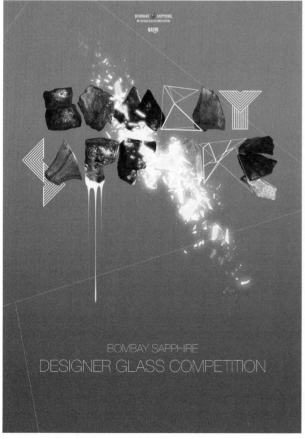

STUDIO: Bleed   DESIGNER: Bleed   CLIENT: Bacardi Norge   COUNTRY: Norway

BRAND REVOLUTION TOGETHER

This is a self promotion project of a brand building consultancy. It is a gift for celebrating Chinese Mid-autumn festival. The purpose is to let clients see the unique creativity of the consultancy.

Once upon a time in ancient China, mooncake was used for delivery of message for dynasty revolution. A paper memo was inserted into a mooncake. Wiseman employed such original concept to spread out message of "brand revolution" with contemporary device - 4GB memory stick, instead of paper memo. The overall visual style is remarkable Mao's revolutionary period in 50's.

   STUDIO: Wiseman International Digitech Ltd   **CREATIVE DIRECTOR:** The Virtuoso Circuit   **REGION:** Hong Kong (P.R.C.)

THINK GREEN

The project began when NHS Derbyshire County were given the task to reduce their CO_2 emissions by 25% by 2014.

Raw decided to create a campaign that was fun, empowering and encouraged staff to "do their bit" while becoming part of a wider green community which they could share information and tips.

The Think Green campaign recognizes the initial conscious thought process and makes going green more than a set of guidelines, and encourages staff to see it as a pleasurable activity.

Think Green aims to mark a new, inclusive approach to carbon reduction, encompassing staff at all levels and creating a sense of community through every level of the organisation. Staff that are passionate about "going green" are invited to become green leaders, driving online content and spreading the message to fellow employees with an optimistic, lively outlook on reducing the carbon footprint.

STUDIO: Raw   **CREATIVE DIRECTOR:** Rob Watson   **DESIGNER:** Tom Heaton   **CLIENT:** NHS Derbyshire County   **COUNTRY:** UK

COWORTH PARK HOTEL

Coworth Park is a unique countryside retreat that endeavors to rewrite the rules. & Smith was invited to create a full identity package encompassing top-line branding for the hotel, its two restaurants and a spa. The identity was applied across brochures, promotional teaser campaigns and a selection of quirky in-room collateral.

STUDIO: & SMITH   DESIGNER: & SMITH   CLIENT: Coworth Park Hotel   COUNTRY: UK

OTTOMAN

Type, logo and visual branding made for a nightclub named OTTOMAN, located at Dunkel in the heart of Copenhagen.

Inspired by the London club-scene, where especially Fabric has marked themselves, OTTOMAN wants to explore new sounds in electronic music and especially within the genre of Drum and Bass. They want to challenge people and give them something they don't expect. This unpredictability is shown through the type, where randomly chosen letters have significant forms. Also, the letter O is designed in different variations, since it's a very central letter in the word "ottoman" - therefore it receives a special "status".

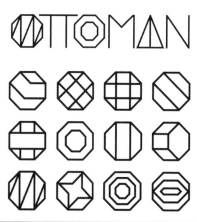

STUDIO: Kasper Pyndt Studio   DESIGNER: Kasper Pyndt   CLIENT: Dunkel   COUNTRY: Denmark

ROITER ZUCKER

With a reputation for radical solutions, Roiter Zucker asked & Smith to mirror their approach by turning conventional branding on its head. In response, they invited members of the Roiter Zucker staff to celebrate their role as part of the firm's tight-knit team and create their own logo using a palette of pre-determined design elements.

The results were placed on the reverse of a large-scale version of the design palette and cut down to size for letterheads and business cards.

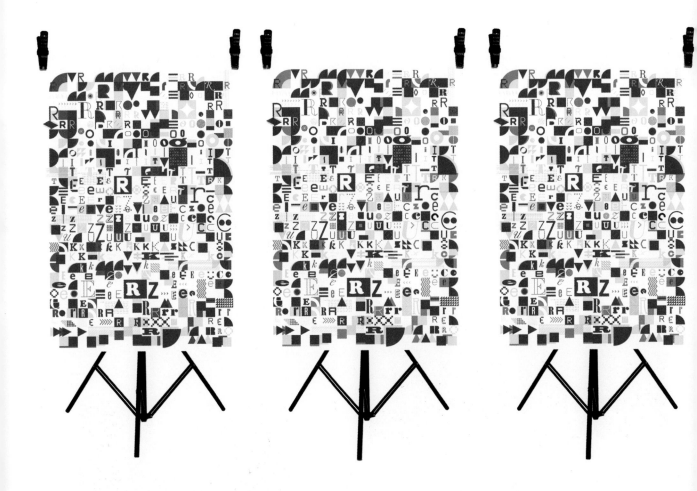

STUDIO: & SMITH   DESIGNER: & SMITH   CLIENT: Roiter Zucker   COUNTRY: UK

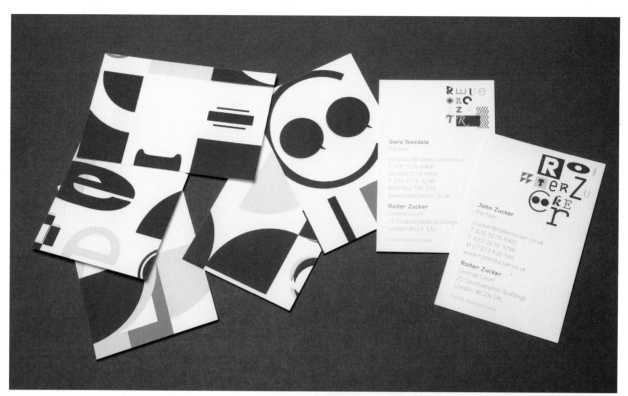

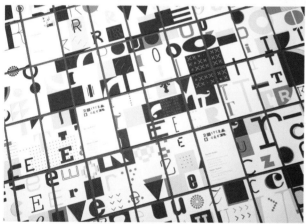

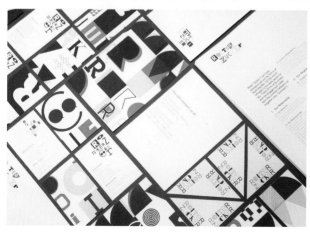

TAKE THESE WORDS

Experimenting with new materials, looking for new manners of designing a message.

CREATIVE DIRECTOR: Alex Camacho   **DESIGNER:** Alex Camacho   **CLIENT:** Personal Project   **COUNTRY:** UK

LE POMPON

Logo, typeface and identity design for a new club/restaurant, based in Paris, France. The logo and typography play on a modern feel but also to keep a timeless approach.

ABCDEF
GHIJKLMN
OPQRSTU
VWXYZ

LE
POMPON.
PARIS

LE
POMPON.
PARIS

John Whelan

+ 33 6 45 75 57 97
john@lepompon.fr

P

39, Rue des Petites Ecuries 75010 Paris France
www.lepompon.fr

STUDIO: Andrew Woodhead   DESIGNER: Andrew Woodhead   CLIENT: Le Pompon   COUNTRY: France

CHILLOAT

In order to create the concept, the name of the product "Chilled Creamy Oats" has been changed to Creamy ChillOat. ChillOat is an informal English term that means relax. According to the concept the fruits are in different relaxing situations. Also the background colours of the landscape match with the fruit colours to make it look like a more delightful product.

STUDIO: Eren   CREATIVE DIRECTOR: Eren Saracevic   CLIENT: D&AD + Quaker Oats
                      Marc Monguilod, Irene Clua   Covides

ACOMPAÑADOS

The naming is "Acompañados" that means accompanied. The graphic solution is based in show furniture on the bottles and different people on the box creating a metaphor of company with the furniture.

COUNTRY: Spain

HYPO ART SUPERMARKET

The HYPO 'supermarket' is a multifunctional space which includes an affordable gallery for art and design, a café, and space for workshops and presentations.

The starting point of the design is a visual language which playfully combines the contrasting worlds of art with that of the supermarket. Silo created a series of slogans inspired by advertising punchlines that promote and address art through wordplay. The resulting style is playful, direct, and easily applied to a variety of formats.

STUDIO: Silo   DESIGNER: Silo   CLIENT: HYPO Art Supermarket

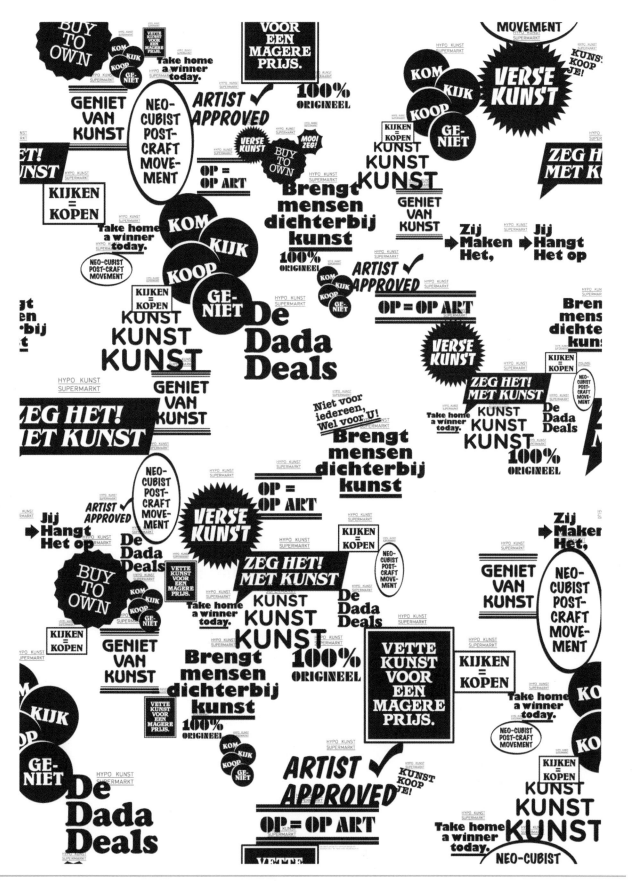

COUNTRY: The Netherlands

DROP INN

Drop Inn is a budget hostel in Singapore. Bravo drop the 'O' to further emphasise the name and also the budget aspect of the hostel. The idea of the 'O' flyer is such that they have dropped and lost the 'O' in their signage. If you return the 'O' to the hostel reception, you will be rewarded with a discount!

DR O P INN

STUDIO: Bravo Company　　　　　**CLIENT:** Drop Inn / Tiny Pants　　　　　**COUNTRY:** Singapore

TINY PANTS

Tiny Pants is a cloth diapering company. Bravo design the name card to mimic a real diaper. The receiver is immediately made known the business nature of the brand. The website is designed to teach people about the benefits of using cloth diaper in a fun and easy way.

STUDIO: Definitive Studio®   CREATIVE DIRECTOR: Finlay Hogg   DESIGNER: Finlay Hogg

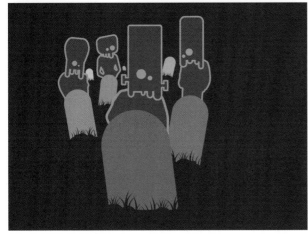

RESIDENTS IN PARADISE

This was an experimental club night and the promotional material had to look unique. Definitive Studio moved away from multifaceted flyer and poster designs that litter our streets and developed simple, eye catching illustrations. The illustrations featured human shaped bodies with masks that matched the particular theme of the night. The typography treatment made use of large distressed letter forms. This insured that information was easily read but also helped balance the minimal appearance.

CLIENT: Residents In Paradise   COUNTRY: UK

COCOTTE

Cocotte is a French restaurant located in the fascinating Little India neighborhood in Singapore. The food is unpretentious home-style cooking in communal sharing portions. The Cocotte logo takes its inspiration from old-style local French eateries and hand-painted signage. Rough-looking weathered menu boards with newsprint menus to further convey the simplicity, the down-to-earth and unpretentious personality.

STUDIO: Foreign Policy Design Group   **CREATIVE DIRECTOR:** Yah-Leng Yu   **CLIENT:** Cocotte

COUNTRY: Singapore

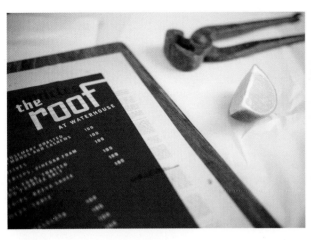

THE ROOF BAR

The identity of The Roof bar is inspired by wheat-paste-glued posters on the streets of old Shanghai back in the days, plus elements from the current architecture of the hotel. The idea of such posters is replicated with the vintage newspaper adhering to recycled wood using a modern version of the wheat-paste-like glue.

STUDIO: Foreign Policy Design Group   **CREATIVE DIRECTOR:** Yah-Leng Yu, Arthur Chin   **DESIGNER:** Tianyu Isaiah Zheng (TY)

Table N°1

Table N°1 is Shanghai's first gastro-bar that serves up tapas-style modern European cuisine. The brand identity is based on the restaurant, focusing on communal dining in a very simple and unpretentiousness environment, thus the use of brown kraft paper & newsprint paper throughout the collateral system. The central theme - long communal tables - inspired the business card to be designed as a little table when folded up.

WANDERLUST

Wanderlust as the dictionary defines is a strong innate desire to travel.

The custom made logotype expresses the feeling of dreaminess, fantasy and the discovery of the surreal landscape of a new world. The dash lines evoke the impulse to join the lines, as with the impulse to travel. The act of joining the lines is also analogous with the marking of lines from point to point, like a traveler would do on his map to plan/track his route.

The airmail tricolor band is synonymous with traveling and correspondence - the conveyance of the emotions and thoughts kindled during a journey via mail.

The brand attributes conveyed by the brand mark are: whimsical, elegant, happy, unexpected yet familiar and comforting. Various forms of ephemerals and keepsakes experienced during a journey were carefully studied, thought-out and deployed onto the collateral set.

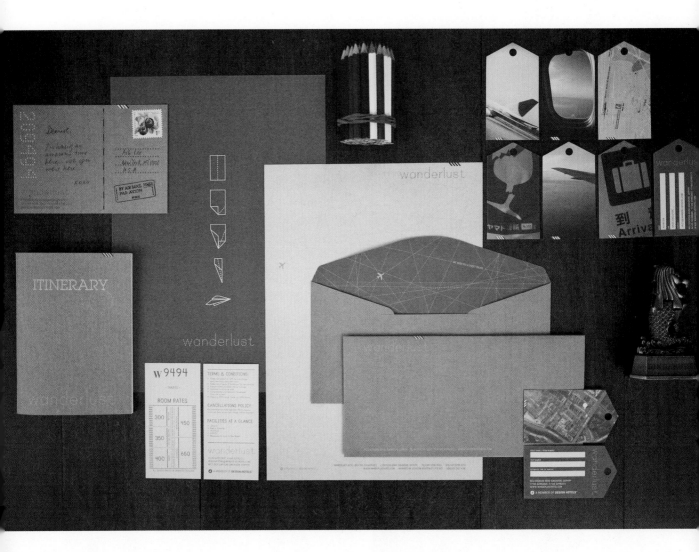

STUDIO: Foreign Policy Design Group   **CREATIVE DIRECTOR:** Arthur Chin, Yah-Leng Yu   **DESIGNER:** Yah-Leng Yu

CLIENT: Wanderlust, Singapore   COUNTRY: Singapore

BIERO BAR

Biero is a boutique restaurant and bar, which offers premium beer sampling, paired with exquisite tapas. The brand identity is based on a bird's eye view of a hop, and the colour scheme reflects the very essence of what Biero is. Biero is a warm and inviting, elegant and classy, modern yet traditional place to be seen and have a nice cold beer.

CREATIVE DIRECTOR: Geraldine Lim   **DESIGNER:** Geraldine Lim   **CLIENT:** Biero Bar

KOFI CULT

This is a brand identity for a Melbourne based coffee joint. The brief was for it to be eye catching and iconic, also having a fun, friendly and modern aura. Kofi Cult is a take away coffee station that believes in quality, every cup should taste the same.

CLIENT: Kofi Cult   **COUNTRY:** Singapore

SKREAM - OUTSIDE THE BOX

This is the second album from Skream, a follow up to his 2006 self-titled debut also released on Tempa (and also designed by Give Up Art). The design concept grew from discussions around the album title with Shaun (Bloodworth - the photographer). They both liked the idea of using a different kind of portrait of Skream (partly as a continuation of the cover that designed for his debut album, and partly as a snapshot to show how he'd changed since then). Taking our cue from the album's title Give Up Art employed the graphic square throughout the packaging.

The album was released in a standard CD jewel case, plus the two formats featured here — Deluxe CD box with an exclusive bonus 'Skreamizm' CD, and a limited edition vinyl box set, containing four discs. Print is four-colour process throughout. They took the idea of obscuring the artist's face over into the cover typography, and other type details – which appear partially hidden on various parts of the packaging. Other executions included a street poster, plus a 12" sleeve for the single "Listenin" to the "Records on My Wall".

STUDIO: Give Up Art   **CREATIVE DIRECTOR:** Stuart Hammersley, Give Up Art   **DESIGNER:** Stuart Hammersley, Give Up Art

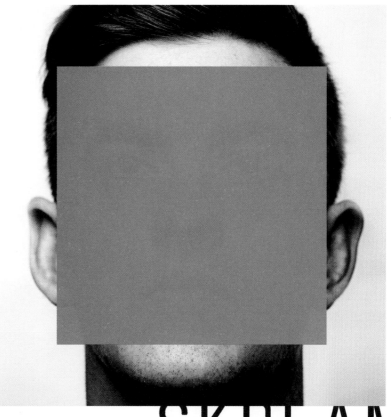

SKREAM OUTSIDE THE BOX

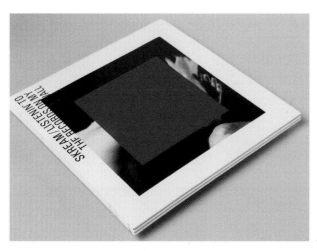

CLIENT: Tempa   COUNTRY: UK

WOWOW - GENRES TV IDENTS

A collaboration between Give Up Art and the creative production company, Superfad.

They were commissioned by Superfad London to come up with ideas for a series of nine idents for the Japanese TV station Wowow.

The series of 5 second idents each related to a specific genre of programme - Music, Sport, Drama etc. - and they played out before each programme on the station.

Their idea used geometric patterns, each pattern relating to its subject in an abstract way, which gently animated and resolved inside of a large initial letterform. Each ident would provide a small moment of calm in between the frenetic pace of channel's regular output.

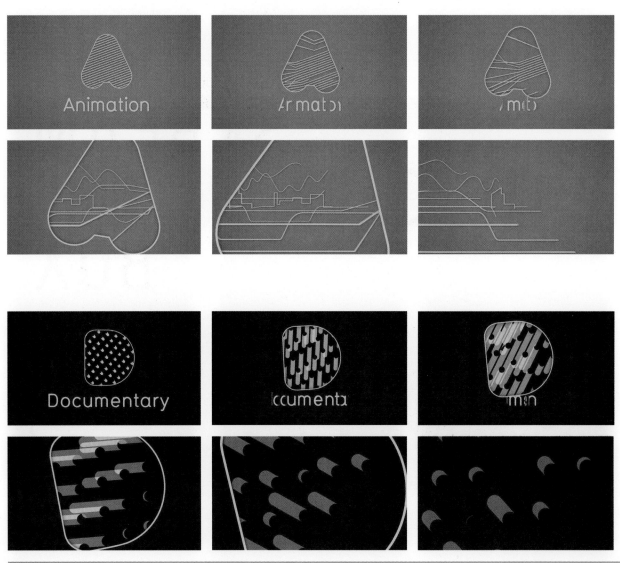

STUDIO: Give Up Art   **CREATIVE DIRECTOR:** Adam Parry at Superfad   **DESIGNER:** Give Up Art

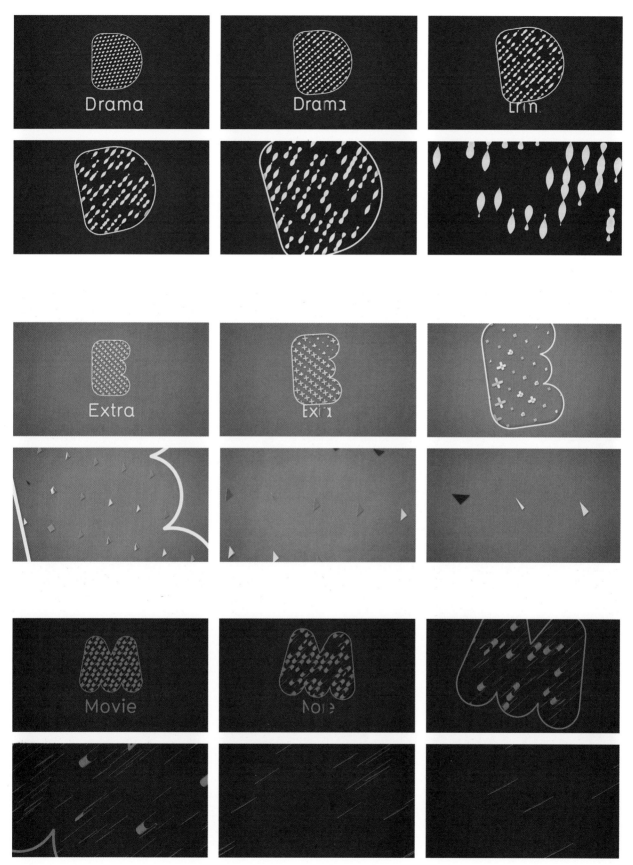

CLIENT: Wowow   COUNTRY: UK

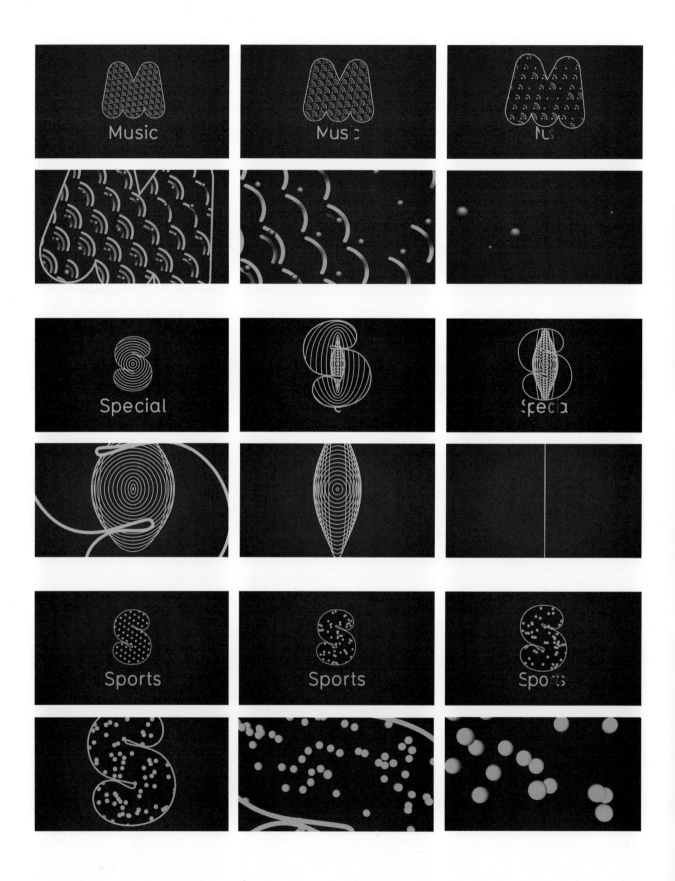

A John Carpenter Film— Halloween.

"Relic"

"Michael

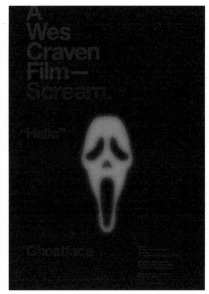

A Wes Craven Film— Scream.

"Relic"

"Ghostface

A Sean S. Cunningham Film— Friday the 13th.

"Jason

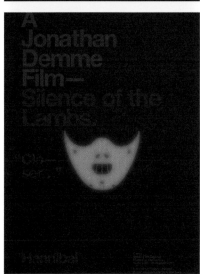

A Jonathan Demme Film— Silence of the Lambs.

"Clo— ser..."

"Hannibal

ARCHIVE

A
John
Carpenter
Film—
Halloween.

" "

"Michael

Creep.
Horror Film Festival
Halloween
15 August – 26 August 2007

Director: John Carpenter
Writer: John Carpenter

A
Sean S.
Cunningham
Film—
Friday the 13th.

" "

"Jason

Creep.
Horror Film Festival
Friday the 13th
15 August – 26 August 2007

Director: Sean S. Cunningham
Writer: Victor Miller
Producer: Sean S. Cunningham

Tickets & Information:
0131 229 2550
www.filmfest.co.uk

A
Jonathan
Demme
Film—
Silence of the Lambs.

"Clo— ser..."

"Hannibal

Creep.
Horror Film Festival
Silence of the Lambs
15 August – 26 August 2007

Director: Jonathan Demme
Writer: Thomas Harris & Ted Tally
Producer: Ronald M. Bozman

Tickets & Information:
0131 229 2550
www.filmfest.co.uk

Creep.
Horror
Film
Festival—
Argento
Craven
Carpenter
Ferrara
Hitchcock
Hooper
Kubrick
Romero
Raimi
Shyamalan
Toro

Creep.
Horror Film Festival
15 August – 26 August 2007

City: Manchester
Location: The Printworks
Theatre: Odeon

Tickets & Information:
0131 229 2550

INFORMATION BROCHURE ABOUT SCHOOL SOCIAL WORK

Information brochure of the municipality of Köniz introducing school social work for children, pupils, parents and teachers. The brochure is applied by several social workers at different schools who personalise the brochures by inserting their respective business cards.

STUDIO: Hahn und Zimmermann   **CREATIVE DIRECTOR:** Barbara Hahn, Christine Zimmermann

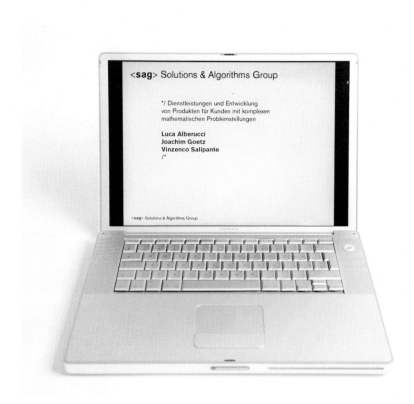

CLIENT: Solutions & Algorithms Group COUNTRY: Switzerland

FESTIVAL OF SLAVIC FILM

The Forum of Slavic Cultures organized a Festival of Slavic Film, held in Brussels in May 2008. The main question posed by this project was how to avoid using clichéd images of Slavic nations. A set of specific letters from individual Slavic languages designed to represent objects from the world of film seemed to be the right answer.

STUDIO: IlovarStritar   **DESIGNER:** Jernej Stritar, Robert Ilovar   **CLIENT:** Forum of Slavic cultures   **COUNTRY:** Slovenia

VERTICAL AFRICA

Vertical Africa is a part of a photography project that will follow in pictures the expedition of a team of climbers gathered from all over the world. The journey's route crosses Africa from North to the continent's southernmost point over a period of 10 months between February - December 2010.

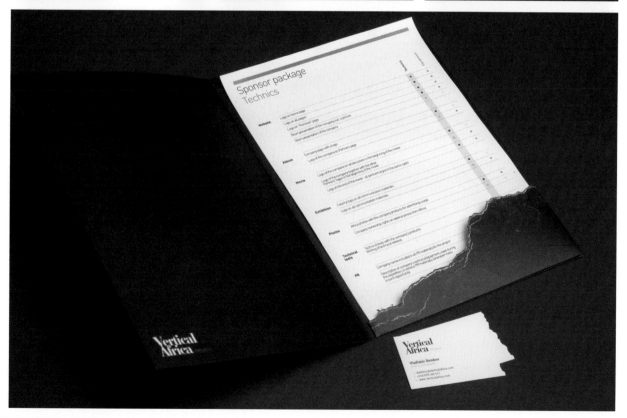

CREATIVE DIRECTOR: Dimiter Petrov   **CLIENT**: Vertical Africa   **COUNTRY**: Bulgaria

THE ROCKWELL

Working with the architects and developers of this new Kensington hotel, Mammal first came up with the name, then created a visual identity inspired by the hotel's opulent wallpaper. Rotating different capital Rs through 360 degrees, they created intricate shapes that appear in different ways throughout the hotel – like a dandelion clock for the "do not disturb" sign.

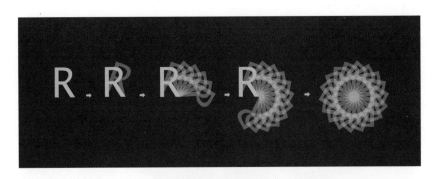

STUDIO: Mammal Ltd.　**CREATIVE DIRECTOR:** Joe Hosp　**DESIGNER:** Kate Stockdale　**CLIENT:** The Rockwell　**COUNTRY:** UK

1854 HERBS AND SPICES

The new label developed by Estudio Clara Ezcurra with shiny black background contrasting with bright and metallic colors, gives the product a high quality finish and an innovative look. The main idea was to translate with some humor signs of universal culture which addressed a diversity of locations, cuisines and regions: the Andes, the Pampa, southern and northern Argentina and other places and cultures from which the goods are original.

225

STUDIO: Estudio Clara Ezcurra   **ART DIRECTOR:** Maria Olascoaga Clara Ezcurra   **CLIENT:** 1854 herbs and spices   **COUNTRY:** Argentina

*Things that are affected by politics.

VOTER TURNOUT

Citizens in the 18-34 demographic are responsible for the lowest percentage of voter turnout. The challenge here was to create a campaign that would engage this group and stimulate an interest in politics. During research John acknowledged that this age range would be more likely than any other to interact with an ambient campaign. Paper asterisks are utilized to mark the footnotes of politics, the message being that the issues are deep. People are encouraged to place these asterisks – which were found in the Metro newspaper – on the streets marking the areas in which they think are affected by politics. The idea was to create intrigue before a series of posters were released, which actually tell the viewer that the most important thing of politics affects is people.

CREATIVE DIRECTOR: John Molesworth   **DESIGNER:** John Molesworth   **CLIENT:** UK Parliament

TEAL

Visual identity and logo design made for a small, independent record label named TEAL, who mainly featured up and coming electronic artists. The work included applying logo and graphics to vinyl sleeves, labels, stationery and business cards. The backside of the vinyl shows how the logo can be used as an effective graphic element.

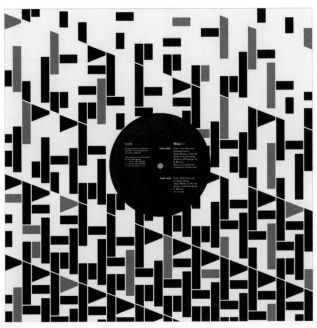

STUDIO: Kasper Pyndt Studio   **DESIGNER:** Kasper Pyndt   **CLIENT:** Teal   **COUNTRY:** Denmark

TRICOLETTE BRANDING

Tricolette, a new knitting shop in London approached KentLyons to develop a new brand, signage, packaging, stationery business cards and flyers.

KentLyons was asked to avoid tired associations with knitting and a more modern approach was needed appealing to both new and young as well as experienced knitters.

The Tricolette logo is made from a bespoke logotype created using 3 parallel lines. This is both a response to the name Tricolette and also as a reflection of the intricacy of wool and yarn.

A fresh colour palette was created using three colours; pistachio, amethyst and fushia. Copper foil adds a flourish to stationery and the shop fascia.

STUDIO: KentLyons   CREATIVE DIRECTOR: Jon Cefai   DESIGNER: Shammi Umeria   CLIENT: Tricolette   COUNTRY: UK

D.A.D.A "DREAM AND DRUNK ALLEN"

About Lily Allen, we believe she's a stubborn and naughty young political activist girl. The idea of the concept D.A.D.A is exactly the way Lily Allen was "Dreamer and Drinker, party animal addicted" still she's an idol (style icon) for young generation. So Mood and Tone of this project would be colorful but a little bit dark and sarky. But still keep the feeling of femininity and pop sensation.

CREATIVE DIRECTOR: Jantamas Nilodom
Chatchanok Wongvachara
Panadda Patiphanprasurt

DESIGNER: Chatchanok Wongvachara

CLIENT: Industrial design Chulalongkorn University

PURE
Against Child Slavery

DON'T TAKE THE INNOCENT OF MIND AND SOUL AWAY
PLEASE MAKE THEM PURE AND BRIGHT FOR THE SAKE OF ALL.
FREE FROM HARM AND WEAKNESS.

PURE

This project made for DACS .

Meaning and inspiration of these artworks is "Don't take the innocence of mind and soul away, please makes them pure and bright for the sake of all. Free from Harm and Weakness" Chatchanok use typo-illustration because these artworks are not only for artist or designer but for everyone who see this illustration. Sometime abstract are so hard to communicate, so Chatchanok use type and illustration to combine with each other and easy to present the feeling of this work for more.

DESIGNER: Chatchanok Wongvachara   CLIENT: DACS   COUNTRY: Thailand

THE MUSEUM IS GROWING

The mandate was to produce a temporary signage for the Montreal Museum of Fine Arts to hide construction areas inside and out.

Under the signature "The Museum is growing", Paprika created a colourful and fun environment by incorporating some objects and onomatopoeias associated to construction into pieces of the institution's permanent collection. They used the colour yellow — one of the Museum's corporate colours — as a thematic link.

232   STUDIO: Paprika   CREATIVE DIRECTOR: Louis Gagnon   DESIGNER: René Clément and François-Xavier Saint-Georges

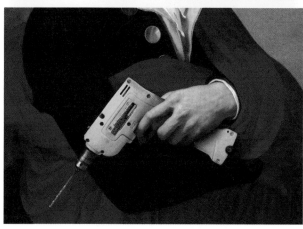

CLIENT: The Montreal Museum of Fine-Arts COUNTRY: Canada

KONTRAST

This final project for the course of studies Information Design, FH Joanneum Graz deals about the conception of a T-Shirt label with the help of the practical example Kontrast, where the task was to combine the fast pace of fashion with the constancy of a brand. Kontrast connects differences in T-Shirt editions. The first issue the "Love & Hate" edition contains two T-Shirts, each shows one aspect of the contrast and a lookbook.

CREATIVE DIRECTOR: Paul Leichtfried   DESIGNER: Paul Leichtfried   CLIENT: University Project

COUNTRY: Austria

SOKENBICHA

Rooted in traditional Kampo technique, Sokenbicha arrives then as the revival of bottled tea—offering formats that balance ancient wisdom with modern taste—without getting lost in translation.

STUDIO: Platform, Inc. CLIENT: The Coca-Cola Company COUNTRY: U.S.A

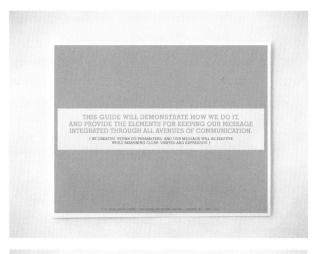

THIS GUIDE WILL DEMONSTRATE HOW WE DO IT,
AND PROVIDE THE ELEMENTS FOR KEEPING OUR MESSAGE
INTEGRATED THROUGH ALL AVENUES OF COMMUNICATION.

{ BE CREATIVE WITHIN ITS PARAMETERS, AND OUR MESSAGE WILL BE EMOTIVE
WHILE REMAINING CLEAR, UNIFIED AND EXPRESSIVE. }

SOKENBICHA

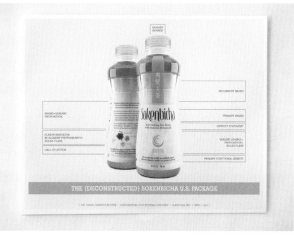

THE (DECONSTRUCTED) SOKENBICHA U.S. PACKAGE

BRITISHISMS

This folio of greeting cards uniquely
celebrates some of those proclivities.
Britishisms is a collaboration with
Joanna Gregores.

STUDIO: Scott Lambert   DESIGNER: Scott Lambert   CLIENT: Self Promotion

TYPE, POSTER AND SHIRT DESIGN

In Euclidean geometry, a line is a straight curve and a circle is a simple shape consisting of those points in a plane which is equidistant from a given point called the centre. These two elementary shapes are the basis of the typeface named fraita which was designed for experimental use in headlines, type collages or any offbeat practice.

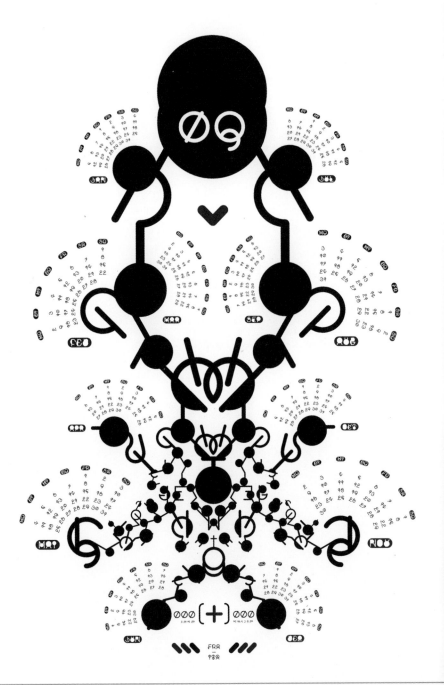

CREATIVE DIRECTOR: Stefan Weyer   **DESIGNER:** Stefan Weyer   **CLIENT:** Buntspecht

LOVE ACADEMY

Since the beginning of 2010, the Love Academy finally brings together what belongs together: love and music. Mellow guitars meet pleasurable beats and a lovely voice adorns the sensual synths. With their distinctive sound these five guys from southwest Germany render homage to love and all its beautiful forms of expression. So it is no surprise that also the band's visual conception reflects this attitude and originates a remarkable and intentional trashy style. There are T-Shirt illustrations in which unicorns are enlaced by rainbows or wallpaper that show white doves flying through sparkling stardust. True to the motto: Liberté, Égalité, Sensualité.

CREATIVE DIRECTOR: Stefan Weyer   **DESIGNER:** Stefan Weyer   **CLIENT:** Love Academy

COUNTRY: Germany

TEATIME

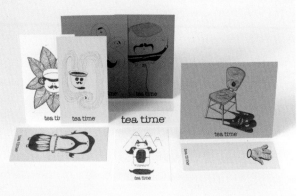

STUDIO: Teatime   **COUNTRY:** UK

STELLA THE HAGUE

Stella The Hague is a theatre company comprised of professional actors, directors and designers who present plays for children, young people and adults. What is unique about the work of Stella The Hague is the fact that it leaps whimsically to and from on the traditional borders of theatre. Studio Kluif is responsible for the design language, corporate identity, invitations, website and other publications of Stella The Hague. Studio Kluif developed a corporate identity for Stella which works globally for the theater company's every need. The S-shaped ribbon runs across all of the stationery and communication devices. Thus creating a unified identity which despite the great variety of images applied to which can still be recognized at a glance as Stella. Clever usage of large format printing permitted the production of very colourful stationery, without any extra costs.

STUDIO: Studio Kluif **DESIGNER:** Jeroen Hoedjes **CLIENT:** Stella The Hague **COUNTRY:** The Netherlands

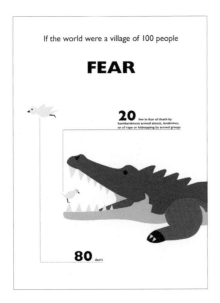

If the world were a village of 100 people

FEAR

20 live in fear of death by bombardment armed attack, landmines, or of rape or kidnapping by armed groups

80 don't

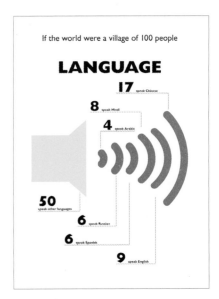

If the world were a village of 100 people

LANGUAGE

17 speak Chinese

8 speak Hindi

4 speak Arabic

50 speak other languages

6 speak Russian

6 speak Spanish

9 speak English

THE WORLD OF 100

If the world was a village of 100 people, how would the composition be? This set of 20 posters is built on statistics about the spread of population around the world under various classifications. The numbers are turned into graphics to give another sense a touch – Look, this is the world we are living in.

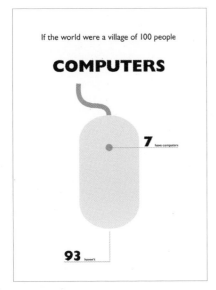

If the world were a village of 100 people

COMPUTERS

7 have computers

93 haven't

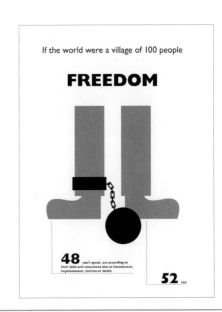

If the world were a village of 100 people

FREEDOM

48 can't speak, act according to their faith and concience due to harassment, imprisonment, torture or death.

52 can

246

STUDIO: Toby Ng Design   CREATIVE DIRECTOR: Toby Ng   DESIGNER: Toby Ng

If the world were a village of 100 people

LITERACY

86 can read

14 can't read

If the world were a village of 100 people

NATIONALITY

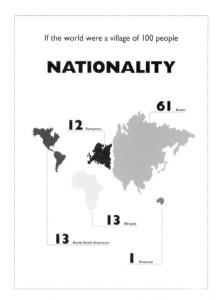

61 Asians

12 Europeans

13 Africans

13 North/South Americans

1 Oceanian

If the world were a village of 100 people

RELIGION

33 Christians

24 others / atheists

19 Muslems

13 Hindus

6 Buddhists

5 believe there are spirits in all natures

1

If the world were a village of 100 people

AGE

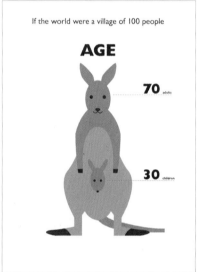

70 adults

30 children

If the world were a village of 100 people

SKIN COLOUR

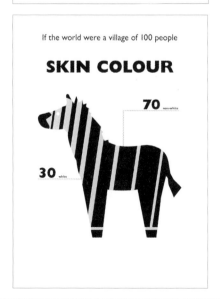

70 non-white

30 white

If the world were a village of 100 people

WATER

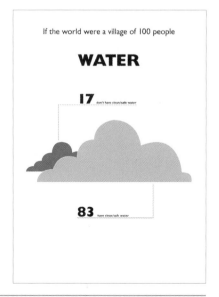

17 don't have clean/safe water

83 have clean/safe water

CLIENT: Toby Ng   REGION: Hong Kong (P.R.C)

ACADEMY STATIONERY

Vancouver based interactive agency Academy commissioned Xavier Encinas Studio to create their new stationery. In collaboration with the designers in house at Academy, they created high-end stationery, using 5 different papers, foil stamping and stickers to show the versatility of Academy's work.

STUDIO: Xavier Encinas **CREATIVE DIRECTOR:** Marcus Eriksson **DESIGNER:** Joerg Merz **CLIENT:** Academy **COUNTRY:** France

THE CREATIVE METHOD LETTERHEAD

The brief was to follow up on the concept of The Creative Method business cards, which had an image of each staff member changing faces from babies to adults using a lenticular printing technique. The back of the letterhead literally shows personality by having parts of faces of different staff members of The Creative Method. The paper can be folded to create different faces with the help of fine perforations. Either amused or happy faces are created every time, illustrating that they always keep their clients happy with a great range of different possibilities. The letterhead always folds down to DL size and can also be cut to make "with compliments" slips. It perfectly shows their work & play attitude and it's a great talking point.

STUDIO: The creative method CREATIVE DIRECTOR: Tony Ibbotson DESIGNER: Mayra Monobe COUNTRY: Australia

"SÓC UN CRACK" CAMPAIGN

Coordinated campaign for Manlleu OPE (Economic Development office).

STUDIO: Zoo Studio   **DESIGNER:** Xavier Castells   **CLIENT:** OPE Manlleu

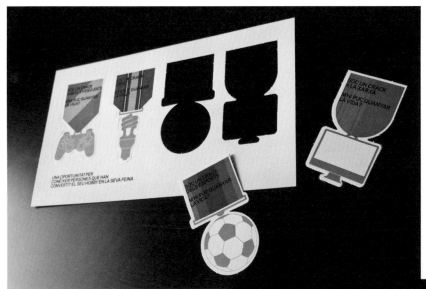

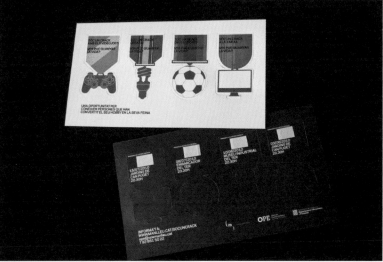

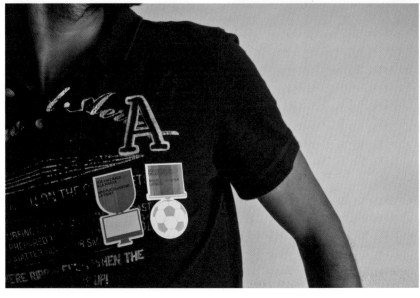

COUNTRY: Spain

REEBOK

STUDIO: Pogo

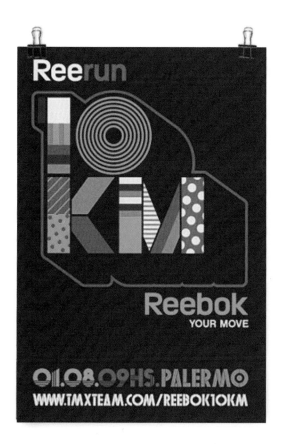

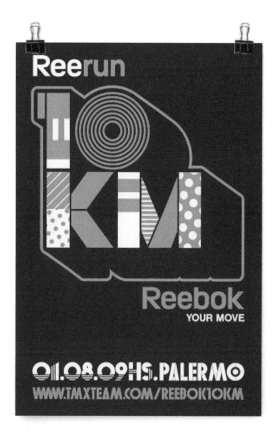

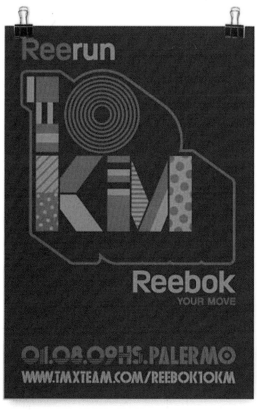

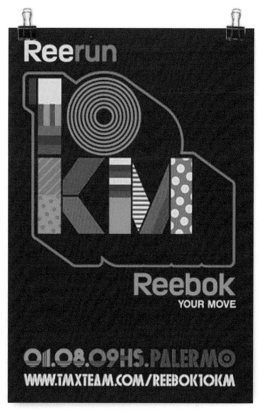

CANVAS

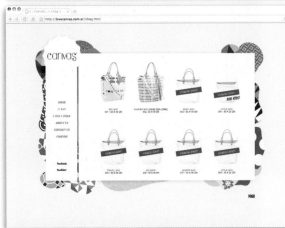

STUDIO: Pogo

NOURISH ME WELL

Nourish me well are independent consultants to doctors, hospitals, and individuals that require pediatric nutrition services. Their core belief is in healthy food and wellness. Company develops its business within the state of Maine, USA.

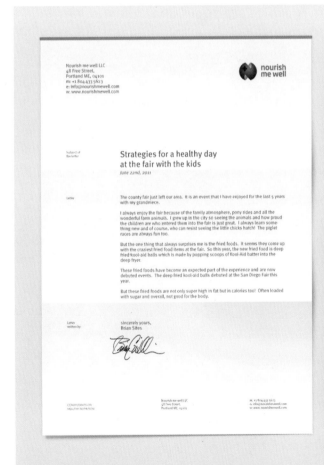

CREATIVE DIRECTOR: Dimiter Petrov   **CLIENT:** Nourish me well   **COUNTRY:** Bulgaria

THE TREE

It is the brand identity of a clothing store. Naples yellow and black present the character of fashion and grace.

STUDIO: 2TIGERS design studio   CREATIVE DIRECTOR: Kuan Yu   DESIGNER: Kuan Yu, Lin Lingjun

spring/
summer/
fall/
winter/

SZIGET FESTIVAL 2010/2011

Promotion for a music/culture festival on an island in the center of Budapest.
The 2011 Campaign also contains a new website (szigetfest.eu) and a serie of virals. In this campaigns Van lennep try to communnicate that a festival is more than music. It is living in a diferrent world.

8-15 august Budapest
Meetingpoint Europe

seven days in paradise

SZIGET
SZIGETFEST.CO.UK

find it at Szig
Budapest. 9~16 August

SZIGET
FEST.CO.UK

www.szigetfest.co.uk

CREATIVE DIRECTOR: Van lennep   DESIGNER: Van lennep   CLIENT: Ostfest   COUNTRY: The Netherlands

CHARLIE PALMER AT THE JOULE

Identity design for Charlie Palmer's restaurant in Dallas, Texas.

The theme of the restaurant is "wind" so Mirko created a logo with circular motion to support the idea of winds and tornatdoes. At the same time it represents "C" for Charlie Palmer as well as a large dinner plate.

CREATIVE DIRECTOR: Mirko Ilic   DESIGNER: Jee-eun Lee, Mirko Ilic   CLIENT: Charlie Palmer Group   COUNTRY: U.S.A

NRC

The NRC Media wanted a new brand strategy for the national newspaper NRC Handelsblad and nrc next. The new identity was introduced with an extensive campaign in radio, television, outdoor, internet and of course newspaper ads. Thonik developed a new overall brand: NRC. In this brand the "guillemet" has the lead. The guillemet is a typographical character that functions as a quotation mark, at the same time evokes associations with the graphical signs for the function "play" and "fast forward", but also to the mathematical symbol: greater than.

STUDIO: Thonik   CREATIVE DIRECTOR: Thonik   DESIGNER: Thonik

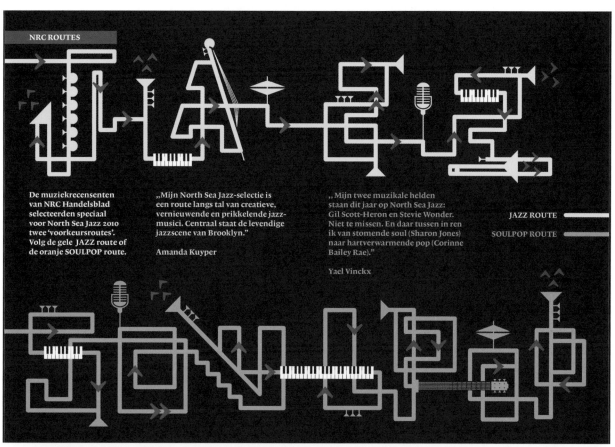

De muziekrecensenten van NRC Handelsblad selecteerden speciaal voor North Sea Jazz 2010 twee 'voorkeursroutes'. Volg de gele JAZZ route of de oranje SOULPOP route.

„Mijn North Sea Jazz-selectie is een route langs tal van creatieve, vernieuwende en prikkelende jazzmusici. Centraal staat de levendige jazzscene van Brooklyn."

Amanda Kuyper

„ Mijn twee muzikale helden staan dit jaar op North Sea Jazz: Gil Scott-Heron en Stevie Wonder. Niet te missen. En daar tussen in ren ik van stomende soul (Sharon Jones) naar hartverwarmende pop (Corinne Bailey Rae)."

Yael Vinckx

JAZZ ROUTE

SOULPOP ROUTE

CLIENT: NRC Media   COUNTRY: The Netherlands

YENKEN DESIGN

Grid background of Photoshop and linear button of Illustrator are full of every graphic designer's work. Many excellent works are made in the same software environment. We pick them up with less decoration and put them in the business card and other studio materials for designers to communicate with others in the same field.

STUDIO: Ken Design Studio   DESIGNER: Yenken Tang   CLIENT: Yenken Tang   COUNTRY: China

ROLLING FRAKTUR

The typeface for this composition is inspired by "gothic texture", which is the most calligraphic variation of gothic letters. While this calligraphy follows the basic rules of manuscripts of the eighth century, it has been infused with a modern perspective and spread across four weights.

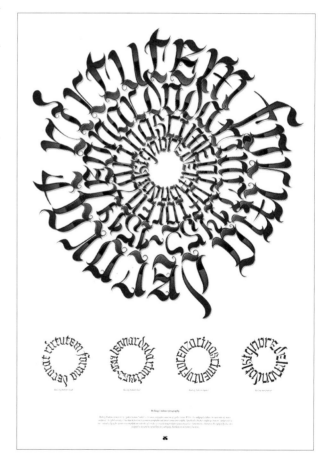

CREATIVE DIRECTOR: Alex Camacho   DESIGNER: Alex Camacho   CLIENT: Personal project   COUNTRY: UK

GYULAI PALINKA/ FIREWATER

The first distillery in Gyula was founded by János György Harruckem in 1731. This nearly 300 year-tradition is carried on by Gyulai Pálinka Manufactory these days.
The task was to create a new packaging design which focuses on the mature young generation. The key motive of the new design is the Hungarian hound, symbolizing fidelity, nobility and all traditional values.

STUDIO: Café Design **CREATIVE DIRECTOR:** Mr. Attila Simon **DESIGNER:** Mr. Péter Berki **CLIENT:** Gyulai Pálinka **COUNTRY:** Hungary
Manufactory

CHRISTMAS POSTERS

The client is an international telecommunication leader who gave Café Design unusual amount of freedom to come up with solutions for creating Christmas decoration for retail shops.

The aim was to cheer people up, make them smile by creating something unusual – however they had to come up with something that reflects the company's image also.

Café Design created figures loveable for both teenagers and adults, using soft colours and somehow unusual depiction. By playing with the perspective – the bodies are facing us but the faces are turned left or right – we achieved an offbeat effect.

STUDIO: Café Design   CREATIVE DIRECTOR: Mr. Attila Simon   CLIENT: Vodafone Hungary Zrt.   COUNTRY: Hungary

A.M.A.E.

A.M.A.E. is an organization that focuses on improving the relations between models and agencies within the legal framework. The identity represents the agencies by a square and the models by a circle, varying its position in each element of the stationary to show the different ways, both sides can interact professionally.

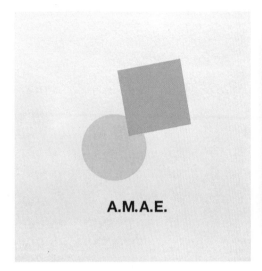

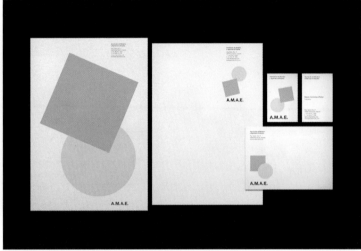

LA FACTORIA DEL VINILO

La Factoría del vinilo is a young and dynamic business project that initially provided vinyl lettering services. The identity, fresh and direct, represents this main service.

STUDIO: Dorian   DESIGNER: Dorian   CLIENT: A.M.A.E. / La factoría del vinilo   COUNTRY: Spain

LA CUINA D'EN TONI

Flexible and dynamic identity for a familiar restaurant located in Catalunya that combines tradition and modernity. All the elements are based on the traditional tablecloth with a renewed perspective that gives to the restaurant a timeless image that matches perfectly with their philosophy.

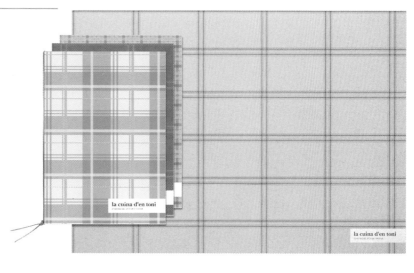

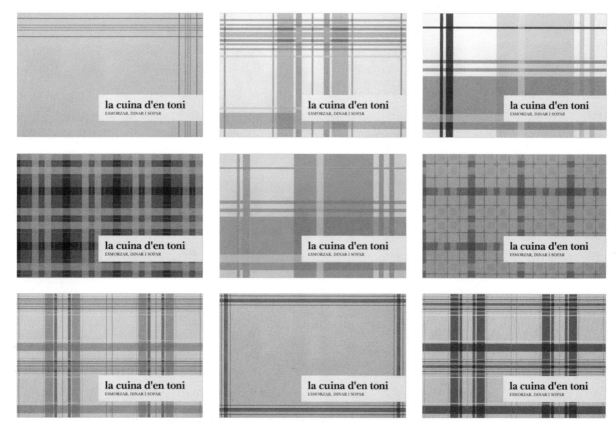

STUDIO: Dorian   DESIGNER: Dorian   CLIENT: La cuina d'en Toni   COUNTRY: Spain

ROCKMEUP

The symbol created for the identity of this rehearsal place and record label is based on the proper concept of music: a combination of melody, harmony and rhythm. These three fundamental principles are represented by three rings filled with different and variable patterns that symbolize the infinity of musical styles.

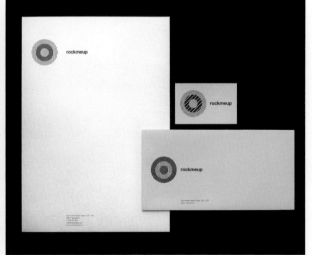

STUDIO: Dorian   DESIGNER: Dorian   CLIENT: Rockmeup   COUNTRY: Spain

OPTIC

For Òptic, an optics placed in Platja d'Aro, Dorian redesign their identity, which had a conflict between the image that was projecting and the high price and quality of the products that were selling. The identity focuses on simplicity and elegance by the use of black and white, combined with a neutral typeface where the accent of the "O" was modified to turn the letter into a lens.

STUDIO: Dorian   DESIGNER: Dorian   CLIENT: Òptic   COUNTRY: Spain

LES PETITES FOUINES

"Les Petites Fouines" is an imaginary detective agency established by a band of senile people in a neighborhood. The four detectives each have their own personalized logos which include an aspect of their personality, like the characters in Agatha Christie stories.

It's an agency of district so their communication works classified ads that they put in the shops surroundings.

DESIGNER: Elsa ANTOINE   **CLIENT:** School project   **COUNTRY:** UK

273

LVNGLOVE

LvngLove is a feeling that transforms consumers' behavior in helping other people's needs.

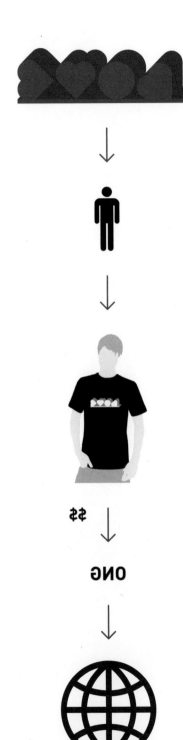

Love Bilbao. Love the world.

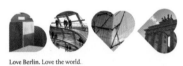

Love Berlin. Love the world.

Love London. Love the world.

Love the world. Love Humanity.

Love Africa. Love Humanity.

Love Freedom. Love Humanity.

Love Dubai. Love the world.

Love Buenos Aires. Love the world.

Love Paris. Love the world.

Love Nature. Love Humanity.

Love Education. Love Humanity.

Love Peace. Love Humanity.

DESIGNER: Juan Pablo Tredicce   **CLIENT:** Lvnglove   **COUNTRY:** Argentina

KINOTAVR PRE-PARTY INVITATION

Kinotavr is the largest Russian film festival. Before the 18th Kinotavr jewellery company Korloff together with the festival administration organized pre-party for Russian movie stars. The task was to create an invitation in luxury style which could emphasize the solemnity of the event. The designs were inspired by the cinema tickets with tear-off line.

DESIGNER: Alexey Malina　　　　**CLIENT:** LeCadeau　　　　**COUNTRY:** Russia

KOP

KOP is an artist meeting place and a contemporary art space. Rob has designed posters for them for several years and recently they asked Rob to redesign their identity and poster to give KOP a more recognizable attitude to the public. Rob designed a very strict grid which gives him a lot of freedom to design different posters in it without loosing the recognition.

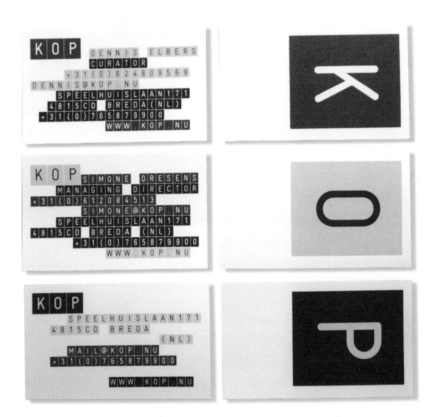

276   STUDIO: Rob van Hoesel   DESIGNER: Rob van Hoesel   CLIENT: KOP, Kunstenaars Ontmoetings Plaats   COUNTRY: The Netherlands (Artist Meeting Place)

CREAS FOUNDATION

Visual Identity for the Creas Foundation. This foundation uses venture capital as an investment instrument that guarantees economic returns and a positive social impact.

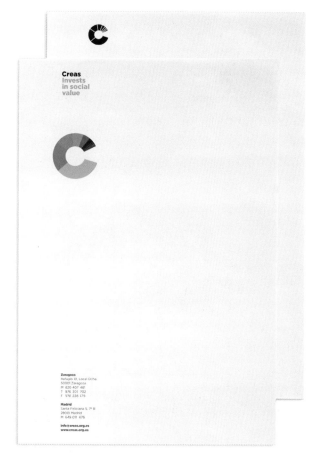

STUDIO: Estudio Diego Feijóo   **DESIGNER:** Diego Feijóo   **CLIENT:** Creas Foundation   **COUNTRY:** Spain

CUTS FROM ABOVE BRANDING

Business cards design for Hairdresser Peter Sokolov. All cards are hand screenprinted with silver on black and black on white, hand cut and hand perforated by Ivan.

Perforation breaks the card in 2 separate tall cards that emphasize hairdressers' height. The first one with Peter's phone number and logo goes to the customer; the second one is kept by Peter as a kind of Rolodex card. It has 4 empty fields for the customer's name, phone number, haircut style and appointment time, so Peter could easily manage his clients.

STUDIO: Ivan Khmelevsky   **DESIGNER:** Ivan Khmelevsky   **CLIENT:** Peter Sokolov   **COUNTRY:** Russia

THE MILTON AGENCY

Brief — With offices in LA and London, The Milton Agency has dominated their field for over 10 years. They pride themselves on a top class professional service - representing some of the most celebrated artists in the film and television industry for hair, make-up and costume design. They needed an identity which reflected their high standards, as well as their unrivalled success in the industry.

A five star solution— Taken at face value, the solution pays homage to the lofty stars of Hollywood. The real action, though, happens in the negative space – a monogrammatic M – representing Milton's expertise behind the scenes and tireless support of the industry talent. The mark is applied subtly across the brand, often as a blind emboss, to reinforce the "behind the scenes" positioning.

ARTIST REVIEW
SPRING 2009

STUDIO: Magpie-Studio   **DESIGNER:** Tim Fellowes   **CLIENT:** Mandy Martin   **COUNTRY:** UK

NATURALLY EFFECTIVE ACUPUNCTURE FROM SUSANNAH FONE

Susannah Fone is a highly qualified acupuncturist who specialises in combining Traditional Chinese medicine with Five Element Acupuncture. When setting up a new practice she wanted a clear and accessible identity that would appeal to a predominantly female audience.

The identity references Susannah's specialisms, which share roots in traditional Chinese culture. Drawing together the acupuncture needle and bamboo shoot in a single mark lends emphasis to the "naturally effective" aspect of Susannah's work, as well as helping to soften the clinical nature of her work for an often apprehensive audience.

STUDIO: Magpie-Studio   DESIGNER: Aimi Awang   CLIENT: Susannah Fone   COUNTRY: UK

MARIA VOGEL

Maria Vogel is Latin America's up and coming fashion designer. The goal for this project was to develop a brand that was convincing, sober, and above all, portrayed Maria's vision, all this without competing with her imposing designs. Based on the first geometric typefaces of modernism, Imprvd Design Agency designed the typeface "Vogel Display" in which they emphasized acute angles and modified some of the characters providing it with a personality of its own.

STUDIO: Imprvd Design Agency   **DESIGNER:** Miklos Kiss   **CLIENT:** Hotel Ambrose   **COUNTRY:** Hungary

RA/NY C/TY STOR/ES

RAINY CITY STORIES

Identity for a literature group which focuses on individual stories and experiences in Manchester.

RA/NY
C/TY
STOR/ES

Rainy City Stories
Beehive Mill
Jersey Street
Manchester M4 6JG
Telephone 0161 236 5555
admin@rainycitystories.com
www.rainycitystories.com

RA/NY
C/TY
STOR/ES

Cathy Bolton

Rainy City Stories
Beehive Mill
Jersey Street
Manchester M4 6JG
Telephone 0161 236 5555
cathy@rainycitystories.com
www.rainycitystories.com

STUDIO: Mark   DESIGNER: Mark Lester, Ben Harrison   CLIENT: Rainy City Stories   COUNTRY: UK

ENVIRONMENTAL BUSINESS PLEDGE

It's not easy to define what gives communications gravitas, but that's what was needed when Mark Studio designed the identity and launch communications for a new initiative designed to recognise and reward businesses doing their bit for their city's environment. But, as you'll see, the seriousness of the subject didn't stop them having a bit of fun with a three-dimensional model of the brand-mark out on the streets (made from sustainable materials, of course).

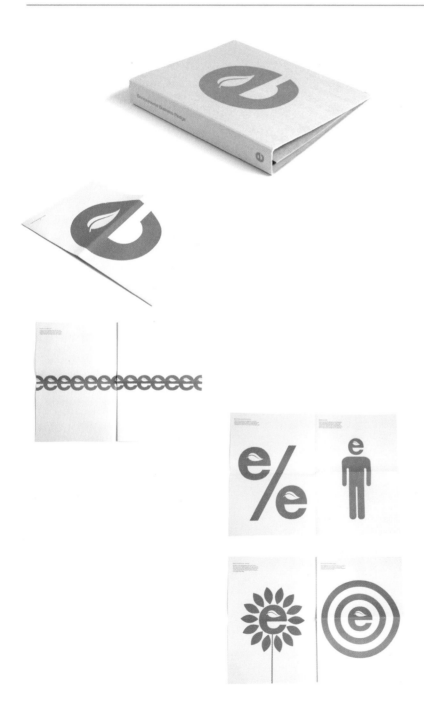

DESIGNER: Mark Lester, Dan Ingham   **CLIENT:** Manchester City Council   **COUNTRY:** UK

EVENTYRBRUS

Branding and packaging for the Norwegian soda Eventyrbrus. They took inspiration from the traditional fox from Norwegian fairy-tales, who is always smart and a bit cunning towards the other animals. The goal was a playful and slightly sassy image.

DESIGNER: Mikael Floysand, Julie Elise Hauge   **CLIENT:** School assignment   **COUNTRY:** Norway

MUNCHACRUNCHA

MunchaCruncha is a start-up business that promotes local "meal deals", between restaurants and customers. Lucas Melbourne was approached to transform a business idea into a tangible working brand. They were also needed to strategically construct communication channels between special offered by venues and a potentially new client's base. The response was a fresh, unique and friendly brand that's easily understood by everyone. They designed a flexible system that could be tailored to suit different venues. www.lucasmelb.com

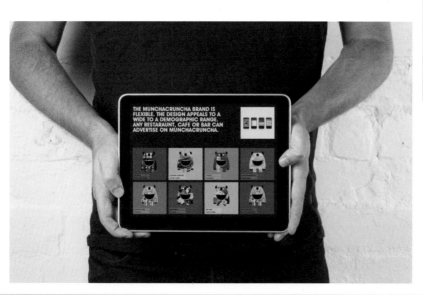

STUDIO: Lucas Melbourne   **CREATIVE DIRECTOR:** Chris Lucas   **DESIGNER:** Eirian Chapman   **CLIENT:** Muncha Cruncha   **COUNTRY:** Australia

DNDC

The Danforth Neighbourhood Dental Clinic is a friendly fixture in the Danforth community in Toronto. Underline partnered with the clinic to create an identity, stationery and the clinic's signage, plus the seasonal window displays that keep the clinic connected with local events.

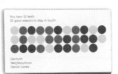

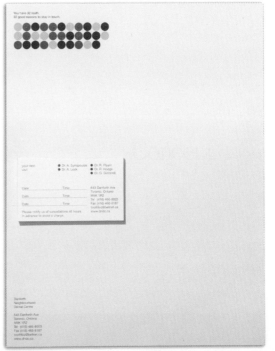

STUDIO: Underline Studio   **DESIGNER:** Claire Dawson   **CLIENT:** Danforth Neighbourhood Dental Clinic   **COUNTRY:** Canada

CBK

The CBK-art institution is connected to the Digital Workspace (DW) and the Artists Studio Administration (ABS). These three organizations all have a linking function. The CBK links artists to public, the DW links artists to digital knowledge and companies and the ABS links artists to workspaces. This linking function is visualized in the "little machine like" design for the overlapping identity.

STUDIO: Rob van Hoesel   **DESIGNER:** Rob van Hoesel   **CLIENT:** CBK   **COUNTRY:** The Netherlands

CHOPIN IN THE CITY

The project Chopin in the City enters Krakow into the cycle of celebrations of the Year of Chopin in an unusual way. All activities have been situated in public space, and particular elements of the project use non-standard actions and modern technologies.

Noeeko was responsible for website and print design dedicated to promote this great event.

STUDIO: Noeeko   **DESIGNER:** Michal Sycz   **CLIENT:** KBF   **COUNTRY:** Poland

1:1 ARCHITECTS

The key to the identity came from the ambiguity/duality that the space between the 1:1 monogram make the letter A - for Architecture. Thus the monogram becomes a symbol of the conceptual starting point of the company - the two founders and thereby the meeting of the creative and the rational. Ambiguous yet uncomplicated and simple.

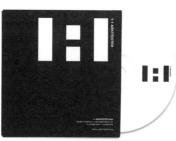

STUDIO: Scandinavian DesignLab   DESIGNER: Per Madsen   CLIENT: 1:1 Architects   COUNTRY: Denmark

ΛKI NΛGΛO

French restaurant Aki Nagao, named after its head chef and owner, opened in Sapporo, Japan, in 2010. Its "Everyday French" concept offers quality French dishes with a casual style in an accessible environment.

Head chef Aki Nagao's cooking style is directly influenced from his personal background and experiences, where he comes from and what kind of ingredients he chooses. This very individual character is expressed with the use of the DNA motif and his signature logotype. The restaurant itself is brand new with a predominantly white theme, but antique objects and old wood is used as key elements of the interior décor to suggest the fusion of new and old. The "Everyday French cuisine" slogan was integrated into the overall branding design to make the restaurant more inviting to customers.

STUDIO: Commune   **DESIGNER:** Ryo Ueda, Manami Inoue, Naohiro Iwamoto   **CLIENT:** Aki Nagao   **COUNTRY:** Japan

T2 EXPERIENCE MULTI TEA SET

Wishing to capture the strong impact that T2's visual merchandising has on the appeal of the various packaging within its stores, the idea of reproducing those rich feelings within a single collection of teas, was the conception behind the creation of this set.

DESIGNER: Sarita Walsh   **COUNTRY:** Australia

MTV STYLE GUIDE 2010

The studio Pianofuzz has developed one of the collections of licensed products for MTV for the year 2010. The challenge was to develop a geometric aesthetic line, such as the sixties Optical Art, but on contemporary style. Pianofuzz created for the collection prints, patterns, icons, and type families.

STUDIO: Pianofuzz design studio   **DESIGNER:** Edmarlon Semprebom, Rafael Botti, Maikon Nery   **CLIENT:** MTV Brazil

293

CHOLLODAYS

Design of the communication
and signage materials for a
temporary Desigual outlet.

STUDIO: Toormix   CREATIVE DIRECTOR: Ferran mitjans, Oriol armengou   COUNTRY: Spain

TOORMIX POSTCARDS

Collection of 101 posters and postcards to celebrate the
10th anniversary of the studio.

ZERO ZERO 39

Zero Zero 39 is a new Italian restaurant
in Barcelona. We've created all the
identity and graphic elements. The
main concept was the idea to mix
contemporary graphics (new cuisine)
with the classics (traditional cuisine).
The mixing is also the type of kitchen of
this place.

STUDIO: Toormix   CREATIVE DIRECTOR: Ferran mitjans, Oriol armengou   COUNTRY: Spain

TRUST TOILETTE INVITATION CARD

Type: Invitation Card
Material: White Tissue Paper, Brown Waxed Paper
Different layes of tissue paper is sewing together. You must turn over the pages for reading the information.

STUDIO: Onthetable srl   **CREATIVE DIRECTOR:** Francesco Roncaglia   **CLIENT:** Trust Toilette / Sintesi Fashion Group

UNDICI BUSINESS CARD

Type: Business card.

Material: White cardboard, black print, white drawstring.

You could read the entire name of the shop "11" when you quickly revolve the business card.

CLIENT: UNDICI (retail store) **COUNTRY:** Italy

COLIN JACKSON COFFEE

Colin Jackson Coffee is a brand new coffee and tea beverage retailer based in Japan. Leong designed all the branding collaterals as well as its flagship store which is spread out over three floors in central Osaka. The concept is meant to create a different approach towards retailing ice blended coffee, cappuccinos, lattes and espressos. Colin Jackson endeavors to serve its drinks in a cozy environment with a strong focus on its product heritage. Each floor is different in design. The only element to link all the different sections in the store is a vibrant color stripe that starts from the entrance and continues through out the store.

STUDIO: The Launch Room   **CREATIVE DIRECTOR:** Leong Huang Zi   **CLIENT:** Colin Jackson Coffee

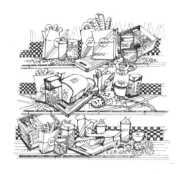

COUNTRY: Malaysia

THE HEALING ARTS

The Healing Arts is a London based collective that was born out of a desire to explore both the collective creative process, and an interest in how ideas propagate.

Lundgren+Lindqvist was approached to design and develop The Healing Arts identity and web presence. In their research, they stumbled upon Anta Karana, an ancient Tibetan symbol for healing. The meaning of Anta Karana in many ways related to the values of the collective while also incorporating the mysticism and symbolism. Hence, they made the symbol the base for the new logotype. The letters of the word mark, which is based on the Replica typeface (Lineto), were interlaced to make it more compact and unique.

The foiled business cards were designed as the three separate parts of the symbol, each card carrying one of the initials on the back.

STUDIO: Lundgren+Lindqvist

CREATIVE DIRECTOR: Andreas Friberg Lundgren, Carl-Johan Lindqvist

CLIENT: The Healing Arts London   **COUNTRY:** Sweden

GIANTMILKCAN

Brand Identity for a 3D motion design studio. The name "GiantMilkCan" is based on Harry Houdini's sensational escape acts. Houdini wowed audiences by suspending reality, and making the impossible possible. That's what the brand philosophy for GiantMilkCan is all about.

STUDIO: Visualism   **CREATIVE DIRECTOR:** Visualism   **CLIENT:** GiantMilkCan   **COUNTRY:** Germany

THE FRENCH TOUCH (TOYZ)

The French Touch is a TOYZ project created by Christophe Pilate, John Benz and NKH, 3 French designers from the collective FROM PARIS. The toy was painted entirely in one day. The idea was to represent the French Touch on the medium with only the typo, entirely handmade.

CREATIVE DIRECTOR: Christophe Pilate   **DESIGNER:** Christophe Pilate, John Benz, NKH™   **CLIENT:** From Paris   **COUNTRY:** France

SOUNDBOOTH

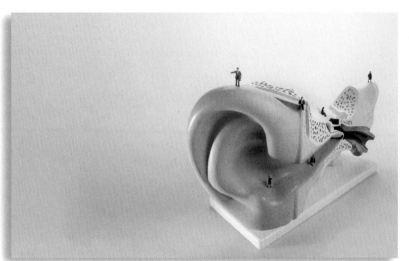

STUDIO: Lucas Melbourne CREATIVE DIRECTOR: Chris Lucas DESIGNER: Jonathan Beach, CLIENT: SoundBooth COUNTRY: Australia
Eirian Chapman

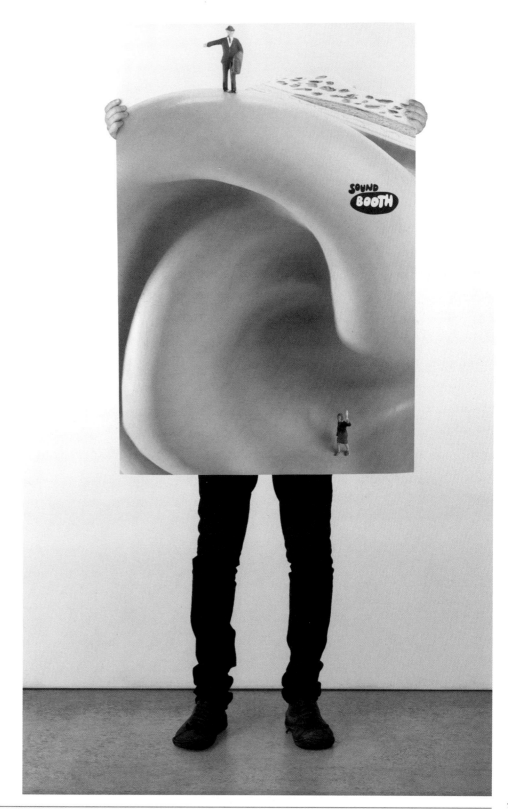

WESTWOOD HOTEL

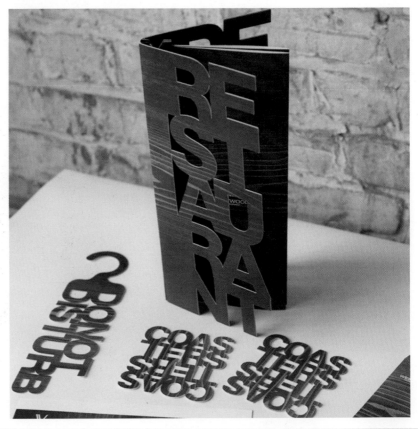

STUDIO: Visualadvice

URBAN GOLF

Our logo for these indoor golf venues combines the letters U and G to create the symbol of a golf club and ball that also looks like the number 19 – a reference to the 19th hole (a slang term for the bar in a golf club). Since Mammal created the logo, they have created a huge range of branded materials, from stationery to wall graphics to brochures with a dimpled, golf ball-style cover, reflecting not only the brand's youthful, creative positioning but the personality of each individual venue location.

STUDIO: Mammal Ltd.   CREATIVE DIRECTOR: Joe Hosp   DESIGNER: Ollie Thomas   CLIENT: Urban Golf   COUNTRY: UK

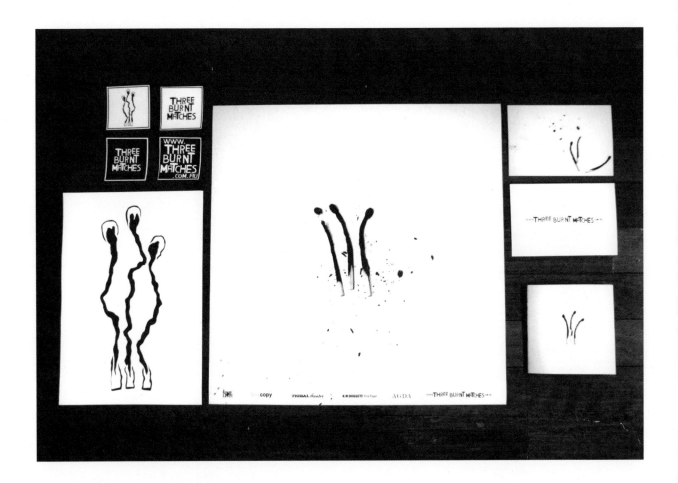

DESIGN EVENT

Promotional materials for Three Burnt Matches Design Event.

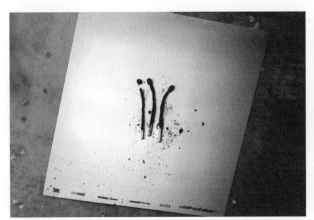

CREATIVE DIRECTOR: Dee Halwala   **DESIGNER:** Dee Halwala   **CLIENT:** Three Burnt Matches   **COUNTRY:** Australia

VOXEL

Voxel is a web and CDN hosting company based in NYC, proud of their transparent pricing model. The folders are blind round emboss on black uncoated stock. The letterhead is printed on translucent paper and an opaque white was printed on the back so it only has a translucent border. The mints are packaged in anti-static bags that are synonymous with technology services.

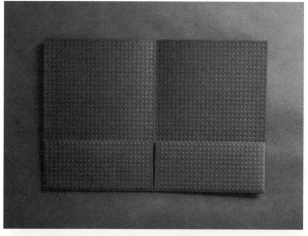

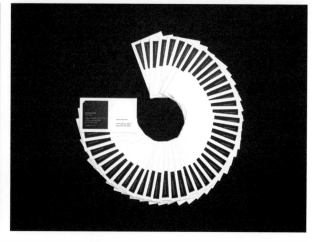

ART DIRECTOR: Mark Pernice **DESIGNER:** Mark Pernice **CLIENT:** Voxel dot net **COUNTRY:** U.S.A

INDEX

& SMITH

& SMITH is an independent graphic design studio based in London. Passionate about the craft and value of design, we work closely with our clients to achieve a full understanding of their business, ensuring that the work we produce engages and inspires their audience. Our work encompasses corporate identity, branding, print, web solutions, book design, signage and packaging. Our clients currently include Dorchester Collection hotels, Harvey Nichols, MTV, Nestlé, 45 Park Lane, Cancer Research UK, Laurence King Publishing and Altitude Music.

Email: dan@andsmithdesign.com

& LARRY

&Larry begins every project by putting the name of our client or creative partner before our own. This spirit of collaboration and mutual respect is reflected in the thinking that goes into each piece of work.
We believe that art and design shouldn't exist in separate vacuums. Be it commercial or experimental, &Larry always seeks to create works that are honest, functional and expressive beyond aesthetics.
The studio has adopted the Eames motto of "Take your pleasure seriously" and examples of this philosophy can be seen in a diverse body of work from posters and print campaigns to our series of Singapore-inspired art objects.

Email: info@andlarry.com

2TIGERS DESIGN STUDIO

Hello! We are a small multi-disciplinary design studio.
Our job is to make things beautiful and fun.
CIS /Packaging/Exhibition/Window design/ illustration.

Email: 2tigersdesign@gmail.com

ANDREW WOODHEAD

Andrew Woodhead is a Paris based Art Director and is involved in Graphic Design, Illustration and Typography.

Email: andrew@iamwoodhead.com

ALEX CAMACHO

I am a graphic designer who thrives on experimenting with letter shapes from an artistic vantage point. While I enjoy utilizing different styles and tools in my works, I view each project as an opportunity to learn something new.

Email: mail@alexcamacho.es

BRAVO

Bravo Company is a creatively led, independent design studio based in Singapore. We work with a variety of individuals and organisations to deliver considered and engaging design. We specialise in identity & brand development; printed communications & art direction.
Edwin Tan has worked on projects ranging from interactive and environmental design to branding and graphic design. Conceptualising Frolick, Loof and The White Rabbit from the very start and working with clients such as Club21 and Levi's. He has won numerous international awards from Communication Arts, One Show, ADC and also the local CGA. His works has been featured in many design books and magazines.
In 2010, Janice Teo, a BA Honours graduate from Central Saint Martin College of Art and Design, joined Edwin Tan and incorporated BRAVO COMPANY.

Email: janice@bravo-company.info

BLEED

Bleed is a multi-disciplinary design consultancy based in Oslo Norway, established in June 2000. Working to challenge today's conventions around art, visual language, media and identity.
Bleed's work spans brand identity and development, art direction, packaging, printed matter, interactive design, art projects and exhibitions.
Both our client list and creative output has become diverse and interesting, and made us one of the most awarded agencies in Norway, with international and national acclaim.
We believe in the power of visual language. Our work deals with long term brand-strategies as well as keeping it fresh by constantly challenging the boundaries of design and media.

Email: miriam@bleed.no

BVD

BVD is a design and branding agency specialised in every physical touchpoint of a brand, in and around a retail environment. Our approach is based on a combination of consumer insight, business focus, ideas and design. We view design as a strategic marketing tool. As such, its primary role is to communicate the brand in a relevant way – and to deliver concrete and measurable results.
BVD was founded in 1997 by Catrin Vagnemark and Carin Blidholm. Today, it has four partners and 25 employees. Clients include global Swedish consumer brands as well as companies from the USA, Japan, Norway and Germany.

Email: info@bvd.se

BARBARA HAHN

Barbara Hahn (*1981, DE) and Christine Zimmermann (*1976, CH) have been collaborating on and realizing projects in the area of communication design since 2004. In February 2008 they founded their own studio "Hahn und Zimmermann" in Berne, Switzerland. Within this framework they have been working on projects in the fields of communication design, information visualization and design research.

Email: mail@von-b-und-c.net

COLT

Colt was founded in 2008 in Clerkenwell, London, as a design-led off-shoot of Scottish advertising agency Atlanta. The simple aim of the agency is to produce work that answers the brief and gets noticed without having to resort to the bog-standard marketing buzzwords.

Email: chat@thisiscolt.com

CAFE DESIGN

We help to make the brands and products of our customers stand out from the crowd. We dedicate our strategic and creative talents to every new project.
We strive for developing efficient solutions that are operable in the market.
We think, and you can think together with us.
All of our efforts are not against quickness, and quickness does not work against quality.
We understand the consumers, or at least do our best to understand them.
We really love what we do, and therefore our aspiration is to develop continuously.

Email: simon.attila@cafedesign.hu

COMMUNE

Commune established in 2005 in Sapporo, and has been active in graphic design. A commune is a group of people living together, but to commune is to share one's intimate thoughts or feelings. A design is not something that is perfected by a single designer. Designing is an act of creation that is only possible when professionals from various fields intimately work and communicate with each other, forming a commune.
We aim to be active not just at home, but also abroad, and not just in designing graphics and ads, but also in offering everything related to creative production, including product and interior des¬ign. The theme of creation for us is to make something better. The act of creation is no different from cleaning or reorganizing a room, and it may have something to do with the act of bettering oneself or trying to attract the attention of a loved one. In essence, creation means thinking about achieving something better, for whatever the purpose.
Inspired by the will to make something better, our design work may move people or it may make society work a little better. It's like giving a gift. We choose a gift with the idea of delighting that special someone. It's a pleasure for us to be able to present something the recipient doesn't expect yet truly appreciates. At times, our creations take people by surprise, awaken their emotions, or even move them to tears. That's exactly what we're looking to create.

Email: info@commune-inc.jp

COMING SOON

Coming Soon is a Belgian studio that creates visual identities in combination with photography. Most of our works are hand crafted and afterwards transformed into a digital image.

Email: info@coming-soon.be

CHATCHANOK WONGVACHARA

My name is Chatchanok Wongvachara "PiNK". I'm studying at Faculty of Fine and Applied art: Creative arts - Graphic design Chulalongkorn university of Thailand. I'm began to interested in art since I was born. I'm in love with graphic design and learn to study digital art by myself. I believe that "Life is experimental" because I believe life is fun and there're too many things for me to learn and discover so I change those attitude about my art to become part of my life and let's fun with it.
My rules are "Life is Experimental" so let's play, let's try and fun.
"Nothing either good or bad, but thinking makes it so" Shakespeare.

Email: pink_cd38@hotmail.com

DEE HALWALA

Dee Halwala is a freelance graphic designer based in Brisbane, Australia.

Email: dee.halwala@gmail.com

DEFINITIVE STUDIO

Definitive Studio is an independently led design studio, based in the heart of the Scottish Borders, who deliver unique and engaging solutions across the disciplines of graphic design, illustration and web design.
The studio was set up in late 2009, by graphic designer Finlay Hogg, to act as a moniker and platform for his freelance work. Finlay studied at the internationally renowned Duncan of Jordonstone College of art & design, developing a cultural and social awareness as well as a passion for simplicity within design. He takes pleasure in getting involved in each and every part of a job, fueling an ongoing dedication to new skills. Every job is met with enthusiasms, working closely with his clients to provide solutions that are not only clear and effective, but put a smile on your face.

Email: finlay@definitivestudio.co.uk

DORIAN

Dorian is a small design and graphic communication studio located in Barcelona. Founded in 2009 by Gaëlle Alemany and Gabriel Morales, Dorian works with big and small companies and organizations, striving to give communications solutions based on great design and lasting power. Specialising in corporate identity, packaging and editorial design, Dorian develops every project by giving great attention to each and every step of the creative process, from idea to production.

Email: hola@estudiodorian.com

DESIGNED AT HANGAR 18 CREATIVE

Designed at Hangar 18 creative (Profession - Branding and Advertising). However this project was allocated to Chris Cavill whilst interning on a summer internship in Vancouver for 3 months.
Chris is an English designer and illustrator who specialises in creating visual concepts to help solve problems in marketing. He offers a friendly and creative service in the windows of branding, identity, packaging and advertising campaigns.

Email: ccavill@googlemail.com

DONI & ASSOCIATI

Doni & Associati is one of the few studios on the international market, specialised in brand design, packaging and communication for wine, spirits and luxury food products. Our mission is to represent the essence of the product and the client company, giving the strength and uniqueness that lasts over the time.
We realize our projects with the knowledge that the image of every product has to be special and exclusive, because the image is to influence people's emotions when they are making their choices.

Email: info@donieassociati.it

DIMITER PETROV

Dimiter Petrov graduated BA in interior and graphic design in the National Academy of Arts, Sofia, Bulgaria (year 2002). He co-founded one of the first and most progressive design studios in Bulgaria - Amity Studio. During his work there he received numerous awards for design and creative. Dimiter is currently working as creative director and focuses on identity systems, branding, iphone/ipad apps interface design, interactive and web design.

Email: dimiter@chadomoto.com

EDENSPIEKERMANN

Eden Design & Communication Amsterdam and SpiekermannPartners Berlin became Edenspiekermann on 1 January 2009.
Edenspiekermann is a strategic design and communication agency located in Amsterdam, Berlin and Stuttgart. We design brand experiences. We start with a strategy, choose the appropriate media to deliver it and then design the complete experience. We make complex information accessible, thus bringing organisations and their clients closer together.

Email: e.overmars@nl.edenspiekermann.com

ESTUDIO CLARA EZCURRA

Estudio Clara Ezcurra is a small graphic design studio based in Buenos Aires, Argentina, a partnership by María Olascoaga and Clara Ezcurra.
Our vast portfolio includes labels, packaging, brochures, web, and lots of other stuff. We enjoy this diversity of projects, people, and challenges trying to find the smartest and simplest approach to each problem.

Email: info@estudioclaraezcurra.com.ar

ELSA ANTOINE

My name is Elsa Antoine; I've been graduated in June 2010 from the EPSAA in Paris, in graphic design.
After that, I did an internship at Petit Pan (accessorize, clothes and decoration for child) during 3 months, now I'm living in London, doing another internship at the agency "IMAGIST", and I'm a freelancer too.
I'm most interested in brand identity, editing, exile, fashion, food and child industry.

Email: elsa.antoine@gmail.com

ESTUDIO DIEGO FEIJOO

Estudio Diego Feijóo was created in 2000 in Barcelona. Since then, the studio has an ongoing relationship with non governmental organisations like Médecins Sans Frontières, Spain, combining with numerous projects of indentity and editorial design for public and private cultural spanish institutions.

Email: info@dfeijoo.com

EREN SARACEVIC

I'm a graphic designer based in Barcelona. i finished my graphic design degree at IDEP this year and right now I work as a freelance in different packaging and motion graphic projects.

Email: eren.saracevic@gmail.com

FACE37

Face37 is Rick Banks, he was born in Manchester in 1985. He is a multi-disciplinary graphic designer who is currently working in London.

Email: info@face37.com

FOREIGN POLICY DESIGN GROUP

Foreign Policy Design Group is a team of idea makers & story tellers who helps clients and brands realise and evolve their brands with creative and strategic deployment of traditional terrestrial channel & digital media channels. Helmed by Creative Directors Yah-Leng Yu and Arthur Chin, the group works on a good smorgasbord of projects ranging from creative/art direction and design, branding, brand strategy, digital strategy, strategic research and marketing campaign services for luxury fashion and lifestyle brands, fast-moving consumer goods brands, arts and cultural institution as well as think tank consultancies.

Email: affairs@foreignpolicyltd.com

FRANCISCO ELIAS

My name is Francisco Elias, I am a Portuguese graphic designer born in 1984 in Fundão. I graduated from University School of Arts of Coimbra in 2008, after completing a degree of five years.
In 2009 I did an Intensive Master in Graphic Design at European Institute of Design in Madrid, Spain. After the master I made a internship in Erretres Studio, based in Madrid as a graphic and editorial designer. Currently, I am working on AND Design Studio in Lisbon — Portugal.

Email: info@franciscoelias.com

FROM PARIS

FROM PARIS is a French creative collective (videos, interviews, reports, art direction, culture & communication). www.from-paris.com

Email : knzo@from-paris.fr

GIVE UP ART

Give Up Art is an independently owned and creatively-lead design studio, founded by Stuart and Emma Hammersley in October 2006 and based in east London.
Stuart is a graduate of the London College of Printing, with a background as an Editorial Art Director.
Give Up Art focuses on top quality graphic design for a range of clients in music, publishing, advertising, travel and broadcasting sectors; as well as working with a number of well-known advertising agencies and production companies.
And we love what we do...

Email: info@giveupart.com

G-DAY DESIGN

G-day is a creative design studio in Shenzhen, China. It has a unique idea of design through visual symbol.

Email: lc9133@hotmail.com

GERALDINE LIM

Studying art since young, I developed my fine art background to be what is current in the design industry today. My passion for branding allows me to create unique and apt design solutions for every client. I approach all design jobs / projects with energy, enthusiasm, an eye for detail. I also believe that lateral thought and conceptual development are paramount to design effective communication design solutions.

Email: geraldine.lim10@gmail.com

ILOVARSTRITAR

Robert Ilovar and Jernej Stritar, established designers with rich professional background and experience from the fields of corporate identity design and newspaper design, founded the IlovarStritar studio in 2008. Their first joint undertaking and at the same time the first project done by the IlovarStritar studio was creating corporate identity for the Slavic Film Festival, which received a Red Dot Design Award.
Both are active in all fields of visual communications with particular emphasis on corporate identity design. In 2008, they exhibited the Designing for the Country exhibition which focused on the issues of reconcilability and visual identities of some European countries. It was held in Ljubljana and exhibited corporate identities of Slovenia, Great Britain, Denmark, Portugal, Germany, Croatia, Switzerland and the Czech Republic. Ilovar and Stritar are founding members and editors of the website media on design Magazines. From 2008 to 2010 they lectured at the Department of Design at the Academy for Fine Arts and Design in Ljubljana.

Email: info@ilovarstritar.com

IMPRVD DESIGN AGENCY

Imprvd. is a small web consulting and media design firm based in Paris & Washington, DC. We are a team of young and creative designers and developers who have one thing in common: The passion for our work! We specialise in various fields but our primary focus is to build well-designed and thoroughly-developed web and print experiences. Through our various client work we have gained a reputation for building clean and award-winning web and other media design products.

Email: kissmiklos@kissmiklos.com

IVAN KHMELEVSKY

Ivan Khmelevsky is a freelance designer from Russia living between Moscow and London. He works in different media, but is always conscious of clients' needs and tries to capture the essence of each project to deliver the best possible result. Ivan specialises in branding, graphic design and typography. His skills have been noticed worldwide and he works with various clients from all over the world.

Email: hello@ivankhmelevsky.com

JUAN PABLO TREDICCE

Juan Pablo Tredicce is a designer focusing on creating identity systems and its experience, for organizations, services or products, working in a holistic and multidisciplinary way.

Email: jptredicce@gmail.com

JULIEN DE REPENTIGNY

Julien De Repentigny is a graphic designer from Montreal living in London. The work of this graduate of UQAM has been published in many magazines, books and blogues such as IDN magazine, design & design book of the year, typeplayer, computer arts, applied arts, esquire (taiwan), nightlife magazine, grafika, enroute, etc. His work revolves mainly around type in graphic spaces and making complex set design environment. He uses different materials to express himself such as paper, acrylic and neon lights. His style can be defined as modern pop art with playful sleekness. Lately he has been working on installations combining web interactions and his usual set design style.

Email: info@visualadvice.com

KENTLYONS

KentLyons is an award-winning London-based graphic design agency. We work on a wide variety of creative projects, including branding, print, interactive and environmental design. Our design service caters to many high profile clients and produces work that is both visually stunning and highly useable.
Formed in 2003, KentLyons creates dynamic and effective graphic communications that engage and entertain. Online, a KentLyons site is instantly recognizable by its ease of navigation and accessibility, combined with a rich and engaging online experience.
Clients include BBC, Channel4, Taschen, D&AD, LV, Booktrust, The Design Council, Westfield and Nesta.

Email: nickie@kentlyons.com

KASPER PYNDT STUDIO

Kasper Pyndt Studio is a one-man-studio run by young graphic designer and illustrator, Kasper Pyndt, who is currently residing in Copenhagen.
Kasper Pyndt works in a broad spectrum of fields including illustration, visual identities, branding, logos, web design, music artwork, editorials, typography and book design. His earlier experiences in design include internships and work in both Copenhagen and Berlin, where he has worked with studios such as re-public, HenkelHiedl and NR2154. Alongside being a practising designer and illustrator, Kasper is studying visual communication at The Danish Design School. His interest for design started as late as 2007 and after taking a basic course in graphic design at Krabbesholm a year later it only went one direction. A healthy interest for typography escalated into a broader fascination of visual language, which has just grown ever since.

Email: mail@kasperpyndt.dk

LI QI

He was born in Chaozhou, Guangdong in 1989, graduated from Guangdong University of Business Studies – Huashang College in 2000 and worked in the design studio at the same year. During these years, he had got a number of awards such as 2011 Sense of Wuhan Poster Exhibition; his works had been selected for the permanent collection by Wuhan Art Museum, Merit Awards of 2010 Hiiibrand, Bronze of 2010 5th City of Design Poster Design Award. His works had been selected in 3rd "Chinese Undergraduate Fine Arts Yearbook" in 2009.

Email: seven_mr@126.com

LEONG HANG ZI

A designer based in KL, Malaysia, Huang Zi absolutely loves translating brands into spaces that engages and interacts with the audience. Trained as an industrial designer, Huang Zi has worked on various projects ranging from retail design, events to products. He readily undertakes all major components of a project – from the initial idea to the communications right up to the build up.
Starting out as an event designer for some of the country's largest events, he has since moved on to work as an art director at an international agency.

Email: fonzi84@hotmail.com

LUCAS MELBOURNE

Lucas Melbourne focuses on design driven solutions. We specialise in the first stages of brand development. That's what we're great at. There are no layers of account managers and finance people and other expensive overhead. We achieve results through direct relationships between smart creatives and ambitious, intelligent clients. A simple but effective methodology, designed to achieve results - not drawn out processes.

Email: hello@lucasmelb.com

LUNDGREN+LINDQVIST

Lundgren+Lindqvist has a wide base of national and international clients that includes a variety of corporations, media and cultural institutions. Based in Gothenburg, Sweden, they work across many disciplines including identity design, web design and development, art direction and print design.

Email: hello@lundgrenlindqvist.se

MAGPIE-STUDIO

Ours is a simple approach: listen to our clients; understand their audience; solve their problems.

We've learnt that it's easier to make yourself understood when you speak in black and white. It helps to move beyond the grey areas and deliver a message loud and clear (or quiet and clear, if the brief requires).

But there's more to it than that. We're avid collectors of all things visual. We're passionate about creative colour – the bright idea that catches the eye, connects with an audience and makes a message memorable.

Email: will@magpie-studio.com

MARK

MARK is a leading, independent brand communications business. We create brand communications that are as effective as they are beautiful.

We are a Top 10 Creative Agency in the UK (Source: Design Week Creative Survey, November 2009)

Our approach

We like to keep things simple.

We work hard to understand each client's business.

We work hard until we find what makes their brand different.

We work harder still to develop an engaging and effective way of communicating that difference.

Email: hello@markstudio.co.uk

MOODLEY

Moodley brand identity is one of Austria's leading design and branding agencies with offices in Vienna and Graz. The team currently consists of 27 employees from six different countries. For over 10 years, moodley has contributed substantially to positioning a multitude of companies, brands and products in a clear, distinct and self-confident manner. Based on a positioning that has been developed together with the customer and subsequently carefully elaborated on, moodley brand identity understands how to create visualized implementations and solutions effectively and strategically.

Email: hello@moodley.at

MIRKO ILIC

Mirko Ilic Corp. was established in 1995 as a multi-disciplinary studio specialising in graphic design, 3D animation, motion picture titles, and illustration.

The studio is especially known for its strong visual concepts.

Before arriving in the U.S., Mirko Ilic art directed numerous posters, record covers, and books in Europe.

In 1991, Mirko Ilic was art director of the international edition of Time Magazine. He became the art director of the New York Times Op-Ed pages in 1992.

With Milton Glaser, Mirko has taught advanced design classes at the Cooper Union and currently teaches master degree classes in illustration at the School of Visual Arts.

Mirko has written several books with Steve Heller, including Genius Moves: 100 Icons of Graphic Design, Handwritten, and The Anatomy of Design. He has also written The Design of Dissent with Milton Glaser.

Mirko Ilic Corp. has received awards from various organizations including the Society of Illustrators, the Society of Publication Designers, the Art Directors Club, I.D. Magazine, Print Magazine, HOW magazine, the Society of Newspaper Design, and more.

Email: studio@mirkoilic.com

MATT CHASE

Matt Chase is a 23-year-old designer and illustrator currently living in Washington, DC. He graduated Highest Distinction in May 2010 with a BFA in Visual Communication from the University of Kansas, the dusty plains state from which he hails. His style, though still in the making, often consists of a visual mash-up between sentimental nostalgia and contemporary playfulness, and his quick wit and taste for irreverence tend to show up more often than not. A constant observer, Matt says inspiration is never hard to come by. "It could be anything from pop culture to an old book in a coffee shop to a dream about a girl that kept me up all night. You never know when it's going to hit you, but when it does, you know you've got to drop everything you're doing and grab your sketchbook." His inspiration for the Postal Service Re-Branding, he adds, came from "rusty old gas station signs."

Email: matt.chase@swbell.net

MAMMAL LTD.

Mammal was born in 2004, when former architect and adland creative Joe Hosp decided it was time for a small, energetic design agency built around ideas.

Craft has always been critical. Never trust a designer who isn't quietly in love with at least one typeface. But as far as we're concerned, you don't even think about craft until you've understood the problem at hand, and have a brilliant idea for solving it.

Design is about solving problems. For us, that starts with business problems. We love nothing more than the excitement of a team brainstorm: thoughts striking off thoughts and the sparks igniting the flame of an idea, we believe it will make a real difference.

Only then do we turn to font libraries, Pantone charts and the Mac. Because now we know what we're trying to achieve. There's a reason to choose that color over this, or that font over the other. It's not decoration – it's communication.

Email: charlotte@mammaldesign.com

METADESIGN AG

MetaDesign is Germany's leading agency for corporate identity, corporate design and branding. The name MetaDesign stands for internationally acclaimed strategic consulting for the development of corporate identity and brand design. Through corporate design, sound branding, environmental branding and interactive branding, MetaDesign turns these concepts into high-impact experiences and brand worlds.
MetaDesign has offices in Berlin, Dusseldorf, Beijing, San Francisco and Zurich. A total of 250 employees advise such clients as Audi, Volkswagen, Siemens, Lufthansa, Deutsche Post DHL, Nokia Siemens Networks, Munich RE and voestalpine.

Email: mroennfeld@metadesign.de

MIKAEL FLØYSAND

Mikael Fløysand is a Norwegian graphic design student, currently studying at Westerdals School Of Communication in Oslo.

Email: mikael.floysand@gmail.com

MIND DESIGN

Mind Design is an independent London based graphic design studio founded in 1999 by RCA graduate Holger Jacobs. Mind Design focuses on integrated design which combines corporate identity, print, web and interior design. We work for a wide range of clients across various sectors; from startups to established companies.
Our philosophy and approach is based on a passion for craftsmanship and typography. We offer practical and friendly design solutions and believe that content and form is inseparable. It is important for us to work in close collaboration with clients, ideally right from the start. Every project is seen as a new challenge and we never follow an already established graphic house style.

Email: press@minddesign.co.uk

ME! ME! ME!

We are not an ordinary advertising agency, we are The Attention Agency. By that we mean, that it's not just about graphics and esthetics but first and foremost about drawing positive attention to our clients through creative and clever communication. We are not offbeat, different or full-blown like all the rest of the industry.

Email: mads@mememe.dk

MARIEVE ROUSSEL

Marieve Roussel is a Montreal graphic designer offering integrated corporate, advertising, promotional and cultural event design. She has more than 10 years of experience in art direction (branding, print and web, events and photo shoots), as well as in consultation and project management.

Email: Marieve@marieveroussel.com

NOEEKO

Noeeko is the working name of freelance art director and graphic designer Michal Sycz.
Open to any form of expression, Michal combines photo manipulations, vectors, hand drawn elements, and 3D shapes.
He worked with a diverse range of clients from large international corporations to small local businesses. Working in the design field since 2004, his work has been featured in numerous design publications and worldwide exhibitions. His areas of specialisation include: illustration, web design, print design, branding, interactive and social media. Michal services encompass the entire creative process starting with the very first idea, through the conception and realization phases, all the way to the final touches.

Email: noeeko@noeeko.com

NEUE DESIGN STUDIO

Neue Design Studio has since its establishment in 2008 created visual communication with the belief that insight and creativity are equally dependent in the process toward creating engaging, long-lived concepts. Working from their 6th-floor studio with its overview of Oslo, they develop strategies; make editorial design, brand identities, packaging and illustration for both print and screen.

Email: hello@neue.no

OH YEAH STUDIO

Oh Yeah Studio is a duo, Christina and Hans Christian. They met at Westerdals School of communication where they started collaborating (and becoming a couple), and doing their 'thing'. Later they both moved to study at Central Saint Martins College of Art and Design in London. Back in Oslo Oh Yeah Studio was established in 2009, and it has developed from a hobby-project into what it is today, a multidisciplinary design studio with two full-time designers.

Email: post@ohyeahstudio.no

OPTO DESIGN

Opto Design specialises in brand development, web site design, corporate communications and display graphics. John Klotnia and Ron Louie began Opto Design in 1999 having met at Pentagram Design in 1992 where John was an Associate Partner and Ron was a senior designer. Before starting Opto Design, Ron Louie moved onto Tom Nicholson Interactive then to the New York Times where he designed the newspaper's first web site that launched in 1997.
In the 12 years Opto Design has been in business, they have worked for a number of non-profit and for-profit clients including: the Ford Foundation, Rockefeller Archive Center, New York University, Booz & Co., Alexandria Real Estate Equities, Inc., The New York Times, New York Public Radio, Amnesty International and Rizzoli Publishing.

Email: masha@optodesign.com

OCD | THE ORIGINAL CHAMPIONS OF DESIGN

The Original Champions of Design is an independent branding and design agency. We make your mission / message / brand / book / exhibit / experience / event / product / package / campaign / website / hopes / dreams.

Email: kinon@ocdagency.com

ONTHETABLE SRL

A table is indispensable to design.
A table to sketch, research, get inspired and create.
We are Onthetable.
Since 2006 we've been offering creative services like corporate communication, branding, editorial design, packaging, advertising, exhibitions, events and interior design.
Communication is the key to express our creativity.

Email: valentina@onthetable.it

PAUL LEICHTFRIED

Paul Leichtfried is an Austrian graphic designer now based in Berlin, Germany. Born and grown up in a small town in the Austrian Alps, he came in contact with graphic design through graffiti and skateboard art. Within the last two years he lived and travelled in different countries and gained work experiences in well-known agencies in the United Kingdom, Mexico, Spain and Austria. Inspired by people and places he is always looking to gain new perspectives within his projects to increase creativity and clarity.

Email: info@paprika.com

PAPRIKA

Founded in 1991 by Joanne Lefebvre and Louis Gagnon, the Paprika studio is unique in its rigorous and exacting approach to graphic design and in its capacity to instil every creation with timeless elegance. The firm is specialised in graphic design and strategic communications for business: identity programs, branding, annual reports, brochures, catalogues, billboards, packaging, exhibit design, signage and websites. Gagnon's style is characterized by stunning graphic themes balanced by a clear rationality that fuses innate elegance to intelligent utility. Paprika has won over 600 graphic design awards, including AIGA, Art Directors Club and Type Directors Club of New York, British Design and Art Direction, Communication Arts, Graphis and I.D. Magazine. A number of the agency's designers are regularly invited to sit on juries at top national and international competitions.

Email: info@paprika.com

PROJEKTTRIANGLE DESIGN STUDIO

Projekttriangle Design Studio was founded in 1999 in Stuttgart, Germany, by Professor Danijela Djokic, Martin Grothmaak and Professor Jürgen Späth. It works mainly in the realm of Corporate Identity, Interaction Design, Photography, Illustration and Spatial Communication. As a team of professional designers with its multi-skilled network of architects, photographers and computer specialists, the studio provides services for organizations in the areas of culture, economy and research. Works by Projekttriangle have received numerous prestigious awards as well as world-wide publication.

Email: jmaier@projekttriangle.com

PARABUREAU

Parabureau is a design consultancy specialised in branding, graphic, and product design. The company operates since 2004, and was launched by two established designers – Marko Baus and Igor Stanisljevic. From product design to visual identity, Parabureau consistently applies the idea of functionality in all its projects.
We approach each client individually, and we base our conceptual solutions on the perfected design methodology. We believe that communication with customers and creating mutual trust is an important factor in all stages of the creative process. Such relationship of mutual trust allows the permeation of constructive criticism and teamwork, which leads to successful development of business strategy and ultimately results in quality products.

Email: info@parabureau.com

PIANOFUZZ

Pianofuzz is a design studio formed by people who share the value of learning and desire to grow. In this context, performs projects immersed in a process of dialogue, research, perception and creation.
The studio priorizes the unusual and clever visual representation, realizing concepts and expanding possibilities, regardless of its surface, printed or virtual.

Email: hello@pianofuzz.com

PLATFORM, INC.

Platform is a strategic design agency that's built the techniques for doing greater things by design. Finding the opportunities where companies and consumers are driven toward common purpose, we build the unifying platforms to motivate both through inspired graphic, industrial and retail design.

Email: info@platform-sea.com

ROMUALDO FAURA

Romualdo currently works as a freelance graphic designer in Murcia (Spain) and all his background is focused in corporate branding, icon design, illustration and editorial projects.
He did doctoral studies at the University of Murcia on the Education of ethics in design studies, and has taught subjects such as corporate identity, editorial design, typography, presentation skills and portfolio of architectural design in various schools and universities in Mexico, Guatemala and Spain.
In their projects, they try to use few colors, flat shapes, and minimum information, claiming simplicity as an approach to responsible and sustainable design.

Email: info@romualdofaura.com

RETCHKA

Nelly Schwartz and Sylvain Gully founded the graphic design studio Retchka, based in Paris. Since their beginning, they work typography, forms and colors with sensibility.
They like to create systems, combine geometric shapes to generate different original results.
They specialise in the creation, coordination and development of visual identity and signage, particularly for cultural institutions.
They install a unique dialogue between client and audience with personal graphic approach.

Email : nelly.sylvain@retchka.fr

RAJMUND RAJCHEL

I graduated from the Department of Graphic Design on Academy of Fine Arts in Warsaw. I have been writing my diploma in Graphics Publishing Workshop under professor Lech Majewski guidance, annex from photography, in Photography Workshop under Professor Roslaw Szaybo guidance. I'm interested in the broad sense of graphic design and photography. My works was presenting on some exhibitions.

Email: RAJMUND_R@GO2.PL

RAW

Raw is a creative design agency based in Salford, Manchester.
We create thoughtful pieces of design and creative communications, with a focus on craftsmanship and collaboration.
Ours is a simple approach: we take the time to get to know our clients, we do all that we can understand the people they're trying to reach, then we take what we know and create memorable, relevant pieces of work.
We look after the people we work with and we like to think that we make the creative process enjoyable for everyone involved.

Email: ruth.sellers@weareraw.co.uk

ROB VAN HOESEL

Rob van Hoesel is an independent Dutch designer with an exceptional career in designing visual identities, posters and especially editorial (book) design within the cultural field. With an eclectic style, his portfolio contains elements of paucity to more complex compositions, where the font is always installed as the main sign of identity.
The work of Rob van Hoesel is characterized by a conceptual approach, a clear language of form and special attention to typography. Simplicity in ideas is the main starting point for design solutions. Rob always works from a content-driven motivation and often with an intuitive design attitude which is constantly measured on meaning and legibility.

Email: post@robvanhoesel.nl

SARITA WALSH

In October, 2009 Sarita Walsh obtained a Bachelor Degree in Graphic Design, Communication Design course, at Billy Blue College of Design, Sydney, Australia. She won a Blues Point Awards from Billy Blue College of Design for consistently achieving high results. On the same year she won 2 other awards from the Design Institute of Australia, Graduate of the Year Awards. Her work has been published in various publications and websites.

Email: walsh.sv@gmail.com

SCANDINAVIAN DESIGNLAB

Scandinavian DesignLab is an independent design agency based in Copenhagen, Denmark with representation in Shanghai, China.
Identity – is our core business with the vision of building corporate souls which actually identify and distinguish, and envisioning product brands that connect with the target, build preference and win the battle at the moment of truth.

Email: chresta@scandinaviandesignlab.com

STEFAN WEYER

Stefan Weyer took a diploma in communication design at the Trier University of Applied Sciences in Germany and received a 6-month scholarship from the Luzern School of Art and Design in Switzerland. He is a freelance designer currently based in Trier, Germany. Since 2004, he has been working on a wide range of design projects, from independent/experimental work for local bands and small clients to extensive projects for companies like Adidas, Axe, Mango, Fanuc Robotics or Luxair. Weyer is specialised in graphics, illustration and typography but also loves to work on animation and motion. His work has been featured in a variety of magazines, design publications, books and design blogs. In 2006, he formed his design and fashion label Buntspecht.

Email: mail@stefan-weyer.com

STUDIO KLUIF

Dutch graphic design hot shop Studio Kluif shows a tremendous growth. The projects, being bigger, bolder and broader, show a great sense of strategic knowledge. With their 360-degree approach on a wide variety of businesses and brands they have not only won a lot of international awards, more importantly, they won happy clients. Breaking the traditional boundaries of 'classic' graphic design they are not afraid to go beyond printed matter and web, eager to take on new adventures. Studio Kluif specialises in everything.

E-mail: info@studiokluif.nl

Email: info@zoo.sd

THOMAS OESTERHUS

Thomas Oesterhus is a norwegian graphic designer. He holds a bachelor degree in Visual Communication from Skolen for Visuel Kommunikation in Denmark. Works include visual identity, editorial, packaging design, photos and typography.
He always tries to aim for a conceptual idea-based solution, where design is not only design, but a useful tool and element.

Email: info@thomasoesterhus.com

TEA TIME

Tea Time is a creative studio founded in 2002 at Barcelona by Sebastián Litmanovich, after being creative director and co-founder of Krovha Studio (1997-2002 Buenos Aires). Since 2010 Sebastian lives and works in London.
Its philosophy is to dedicate all the care and know-how to develop every project with one clear goal - to achieve great results in both commercial and creative terms, devising strong concepts and great results for graphic design, art direction, branding, packaging, editorial design and more.
Tea Time = Conceptual + clean + timeless.

Email: aloha@teatimestudio.com

TOORMIX

Toormix is a Barcelona-based design studio specialising in branding, art direction, creativity and graphic design, set up in 2000 by Ferran Mitjans and Oriol Armengou. We carry out corporate identity, editorial, print, web and communication projects for a wide variety of clients, from small graphic pieces to global branding and communication projects.
Our way of working is based around strategic collaboration with the client. Starting from information and ideas, we develop a clear and coherent creative discourse in order to reach people through innovative and visually attractive design proposals.

Email: oriol@toormix.com

THONIK

Thonik designs visual communication. The firm was founded in 1993 by Thomas Widdershoven and Nikki Gonnissen. Currently there are fifteen employees.
Initially Thonik concentrated on the cultural sector (publishers, architects, museums, cultural trusts and events). Since 2003 its operations have extended to organizations involved in politics and administration. Thonik won its first major order in the commercial sector in 2008.
Recent clients include Museum Boijmans van Beuningen, the 2008 Venice Architecture Biennial, the Dutch Socialist Party (SP), Amsterdam Public Library and Triodos Bank.

Email: Danielle@thonik.nl

TOBY NG

Toby Ng graduated in Graphic Design from Central St. Martin's, London in 2008 and is now stationed in Hong Kong with Sandy Choi Associates. Ng's designs have received global recognition including the Red Dot Awards, GDC Awards, International Design Awards and the HOW International Design Awards. In Jan 2010, Toby has been named as "Young Asian 36 Designers" by Korean design magazine Designnet. His photographs were shortlisted for The Taylor Wessing Photographic Portrait Prizes 2008 and exhibited in the National Portrait Gallery, London and various national galleries in the UK.

Email: mail@toby-ng.com

TYPE FABRIC

Type Fabric consists of Catrina Wipf and Samuel Egloff from Lucerne, Switzerland.
After studying Graphic Design together, the studio Type Fabric was founded right away in summer 2009. In summer 2010 we additionally became part of Edition Typoundso, a self-publishing group.

Email: info@typefabric.ch

TRULY DEEPLY

We are obsessive about creating brands that evoke powerful emotional connections with customers.
We unlock the magic of creating outstanding brand expressions that are born out of deep strategic insights, communicating on brand and on message. This seamless process reveals our creatives to be strategic brand thinkers, as well as masters of their creative craft.
We succeed only when your brand 'truly deeply' connects with your customers and if that requires adding a little 'madness' to the equation, then we're up for that as well.
We deliver the most powerful and compelling brand platforms, distilling organizational conversations, market immersion and research into telling insight.

Email : lachlan@trulydeeply.com.au

THE CREATIVE METHOD

The Creative Method was established in October of 2005 and was built from the desire to create a world class design studio out of Sydney.
The philosophy is simple, to produce the greatest ideas with the best possible execution. It's a ongoing work in progress and involves constantly pushing ourselves, our clients, the mediums we works within and ultimately the consumers.
The Creative Method has won a number of awards both nationally and internationally and has featured in a mountain of publications globally. Whilst recognition of our design peers is great.
Our client base covers large global corporate down to small start up businesses. Work disciplines include, consumer branding and packaging, brand creation, development and experience, new media and advertising. Essentially anything that requires a great idea to generate brand traction.

E-mail: tony@thecreativemethod.com

UNIFORM STRATEGIC DESIGN

Uniform is a multidisciplinary strategic design consultancy from Oslo, Norway. We work within a wide range of projects, from corporate identities, interactive websites, magazines, books and packaging. We believe that strong concept and a unique brand story enhances and strengthens the identity. Our heart beats especially for brands that are sustainable and ecological.

Email: Ludvig@uniform.no

UNDERLINE STUDIO

Underline Studio is a design firm based in Toronto that specialises in classic, sophisticated design. Underline has gained international recognition for creating intelligent and engaging design solutions for clients such as Dyson Canada, Harry Rosen, the Young Centre for the Performing Arts, the University of Toronto, Prefix Institute of Contemporary Art and Random House Canada.

Email: info@underlinestudio.com

VISUALISM

We are Visualism – a multidisciplinary design studio based in Hamburg, Germany with a focus on visual communication, brand identity, art-direction and illustration.
Coming from various subcultures, we keep a playful and experimental approach to our work while maintaining an equally professional attitude. The foundation for all of our projects is rooted in solid strategic thinking and a strong yet organic, conceptual process.

Email: jan@visualism.de

VIKTOR KONOVALOV

Viktor Konovalov (K. Love) - partner and creative director of the SuperHeroes branding agency, CMO of Green Battery Inc. (innovations in solar energy).

Email: ceo@xclv.com

WALLNUT STUDIO

Founded in 2007, Wallnut is a graphic design, textile and branding studio specialising in interdisciplinary projects. Run by Colombian graphic designer, Cristina Londoño, it has a reputation for generating contemporary works developed from a profound passion for color, an obsession for detail and a lust for research, all applied to concepts, surfaces, fashion, prints and interiors among others.

Email: info@wallnutstudio.com

WISEMAN

Wiseman is a brand building consultancy which was established since 2001. We cooperate with clients to upgrade value of their business through building up brands.
We create rich and special brand experiences through extraordinary creativity and strategic insight. We intent to build a long-term trust affinity with brand owner in order to create unique bond between brand and target audience.

Email: info@wisemanhk.com

XAVIER ENCINAS STUDIO

Known to push the boundaries in print production, Xavier Encinas Studio specialises in editorial design and print collateral.
From conception to production, we strive to create work that is aesthetically beautiful, simple yet clever.
Our experience paired with a healthy obsession for high-end materials and printing techniques, ensures a distinctively crafted product.
Since 2005, the studio has enjoyed working for renowned international brands as well as independents and those who are just getting started. We collaborate with innovative photographers, graphic designers and illustrators to meet the needs of a diverse range of clients and execute large-scale projects.
Xavier Encinas Studio is based in Paris.

Email: hello@xavierencinas.com

YENKEN TANG

Graphic Designer, Creative Director of Shenzhen Ken Design Office, Member of Shenzhen Graphic Design Association (SGDA). Committed to explore the value of visual design in the community, business and academic value of unity and diversity. Covers the work of shaping the brand and corporate image, advertising and promotion of design and other fields, in order to service and consumer brands, culture and creative industries, enterprises and government agencies, etc. to provide design services in many industries.

Email: yenken@163.com

ZAZDESIGN GRAPHIC LAB

Zazdesign graphic lab is a design studio situated in Athens/Greece founded in 2008 and is run by two passionate sisters Daria & Zinaida Zaziret. We are all about fresh & creative concepts. We love to think "outside the box" without limitations and are obsessed with focusing on details. The most important thing in our approach is a well thought-out idea, which always lies in the base of project creation.

Email: daria@zazdesign.gr

ZOO STUDIO

Zoo Studio is a design studio located in Barcelona created by 4 professionals from different areas and at the same time complementary as graphic design, multimedia design, music production and video. This multidisciplinary character is extended to the other members of the team, and it allows us to give an innovative view to any project, either by packaging design, web environment or in a global corporate identity project.

Email: info@zoo.ad